# Rights vs. Public Safety after 9/11

**Rights and Responsibilities:**
**Communitarian Perspectives**
Series Editor: Amitai Etzioni

# Rights vs. Public Safety after 9/11

## America in the Age of Terrorism

EDITED BY
AMITAI ETZIONI AND JASON H. MARSH

ROWMAN & LITTLEFIELD PUBLISHERS, INC.
*Lanham • Boulder • New York • Oxford*

ROWMAN & LITTLEFIELD PUBLISHERS, INC. Kennedy School Library

Published in the United States of America
by Rowman & Littlefield Publishers, Inc.
A Member of the Rowman & Littlefield Publishing Group
4501 Forbes Boulevard, Suite 200, Lanham, Maryland 20706
www.rowmanlittlefield.com

PO Box 317
Oxford
OX2 9RU, UK

British Library Cataloguing in Publication Information Available

**Library of Congress Cataloging-in-Publication Data**

Etzioni, Amitai.
  Rights vs. public safety after 9/11 : America in the age of terrorism / Amitai
Etzioni, Jason H. Marsh
      p. cm. — (Rights and responsibilities : communitarian perspectives)
    Includes bibliographical references and index.
    ISBN 0-7425-2754-9 (cloth : alk. paper) — ISBN 0-7425-2755-7 (pbk. : alk.
paper)
    1. Terrorism—Prevention—Government policy—United States. 2. Civil
rights—United States. I. Marsh, Jason H., 1977– II. Title. III. Rights and
responsibilities (Lanham, Md.).
  HV6432 .E88 2003
  363.3'2'0973—dc21

                                                                    2002012832

Printed in the United States of America.

∞™ The paper used in this publication meets the minimum requirements of
American National Standard for Information Sciences—Permanence of Paper
for Printed Library Materials, ANSI/NISO Z39.48-1992.

# CONTENTS

## PART II   THE SPECIFICS

### Immigration

### Racial Profiling

### Freedom of the Press versus National Security

### Public Health

### A Just War?

## National Service

## PART III   AMERICAN SOCIETY AFTER SEPTEMBER 11

# INTRODUCTION: RIGHTS AND RESPONSIBILITIES, POST 9/11

## Amitai Etzioni

**D**iscussions of matters concerning public affairs are often couched in terms acquired from our legal culture. The implicit assumption is that both sides (rarely is there room for more) will state their position like lawyers in court, in the starkest possible way, drawing on whatever arguments they can marshal, even if these greatly distort the facts and vastly misrepresent the other side. In yesterday's America, in the world before September 11, civil rights and public safety were often discussed in this way. On the one side, libertarians made strong, uncompromising cases for liberty. In effect, practically any suggestions made in the name of shoring up our safety, including the antiterrorism measures urged on the country by a 1996 commission on national security, were severely criticized as unnecessary invasions of our freedoms. The government (a.k.a. Big Brother), not terror, was considered the main threat to liberty. On the other side, the political right characterized the American Civil Liberties Union (ACLU) and its generally liberal sister organizations as undermining the moral fabric of the country, destroying its social order, and inviting terrorism.

In the weeks that followed September 11, the country pulled together. A strong spirit of community prevailed. Bipartisanship governed.

Differences were not suppressed, but they were worked out. Posturing was replaced largely by a competition for who could do more and better for the nation by working with the other side. Congress—working with the White House—sorted out where the new point of balance would be between our all-too-evident need to enhance public safety (especially facing the threat of terrorists using weapons of mass destruction) and our profound commitment to respect and uphold our rights.

The old habits did not disappear. There were those who argued that practically any measure aimed at protecting the homeland was going to "shred the Constitution" and "do the terrorists' work for them." Others argued that Americans' lifestyles had brought this crisis on them. Jerry Falwell pointed a finger at "the pagans, and the abortionists, and the feminists, and the gays and the lesbians who are actively trying to make that an alternative lifestyle, the ACLU, People for the American Way, all of them who have tried to secularize America."[1] But, as illustrated by the key documents that opened the public policy deliberations—the administration's position outlined by Attorney General John Ashcroft and the counterproposal by Democratic Senator Patrick Leahy (chapters 1 and 2, respectively)—the main representatives of both sides lowered their voices and moved toward one another, ultimately passing the USA Patriot Act in record time (chapter 4 provides a summary of the Patriot Act). Although differences continue to exist, as they ought to, they are expressed in terms that leave the door open to civil dialogues, productive exchanges, and reasonable policies mindful of both safety and rights. This was illustrated in the debate over military tribunals, where the White House's original proposal was tempered in the final order issued by the Department of Defense (also in chapter 4).

## THE BALANCE

The Constitution has always been a living document and has been adapted to the changing needs of the times—a point emphasized by Judge Richard Posner in chapter 5. This is evident if we recall that until the ACLU reinterpreted the First Amendment in the 1920s, it was hardly a steely protector of free speech. More dramatically, if we were to rely on the unchanging text of the Constitution, then of course we would have no right of privacy, which the Constitution does not even mention; we must recall that privacy is a right fashioned as recently as 1965! If we can create a whole new right out of the penumbra of the Constitution, we surely can refashion it some, not because we have just experienced the most devastating attack on our homeland ever, but because we face the prospect of more and worse.

Even if we were to stick merely to the Founding Fathers' text, the governing Fourth Amendment is not phrased in the absolute way the First Amendment is. It does not state that Congress "shall make no law allowing search and seizure" or anything remotely like that. It states that there be no *un*reasonable searches. It is one of only two rights-defining amendments that recognize, on the face of it, the importance of taking into account the public interest. Indeed, the courts have long recognized that our right to privacy must be weighed against our need for public safety (and public health).

The next step is to draw on this very general principle for more specific guidance as to when to give priority to privacy and when to public safety. Meeting major new challenges as they arise provides one criterion. Thus, when new privacy-invading technologies have been developed over recent years, we introduced massive new regulations to protect medical privacy and some to enhance financial privacy. Now there is a massive new threat to public safety that deserves new consideration.

Next, as we introduce new safety measures, we ought to focus on those that are minimally intrusive and highly productive in terms of public protection and avoid those that have the opposite profile. It is perfectly reasonable to argue that if we allow public authorities—after they obtain a warrant—to tap phones and open mail, we shall also enable and allow them to monitor e-mail and read encrypted messages. As we allow police to scan crowds in public spaces, so we should allow computers.

Moreover, once we put our mind to it, we can reduce the clash between the need for safety and the traditional formulation of our rights. Civil libertarians have opposed devices that allow authorities to pinpoint places from which people make cell phone calls. Rescuers find them very useful. Let's add an on/off switch. The ACLU opposed the introduction at airports of x-ray machines that can determine whether people are carrying concealed weapons under their clothes. (Barry Steinhardt, associate director of the ACLU, stated that he fears custom agents could see you in your birthday suit—and put the pictures on the Internet.) Maybe now the ACLU will find these devices tolerable once it notes that in order to be scanned, people need to sign a consent form and that the pictures are quite opaque.

At the same time, it is repugnant even to talk about detaining Arab Americans the way we did Japanese Americans during World War II. Requiring all Americans to carry government-issued ID cards at all times and stopping people at random to demand identification, common in Europe, is another measure that is both a gross violation of our basic rights and contributes very little to public safety.

Still other measures may require considerable deliberation. Stopping and questioning all Arab Americans constitutes a massive violation of privacy and does little for public safety other than squander police and FBI resources. However, paying special attention to young males with new flight licenses seeking to travel on a major airline who seem Middle Eastern may be a kind of profiling that is justifiable. It seems to meet the criteria often used by law: it is what a reasonable person would find, well, reasonable.

In all such deliberations, it is crucial to note that nations have not lost their liberty as a result of a small accumulation of increased safety measures that pushed them down a slippery slope to the unraveling of their constitutional rights; they lost their freedoms when public authorities failed to respond to urgent public needs. We face a major new challenge. To argue that most any strengthening of the devices and procedures used by public authorities to enhance public safety would "drive a stake through the heart of the Constitution" or "make us do the terrorists' job for them by turning us into a people like them" is going to stand in the way of engaging in carefully reasoned deliberations about how far we should go—and where no terrorists should make us dare to tread. (Harvard law professor Laurence Tribe discusses these issues in chapter 3.)

## THE SPECIFICS

Reasonable people can differ on the specific issues that are at stake. Sometimes there is room for true alarm. When the administration suggested that immigrants should be able to be detained, without being charged or tried, for "indefinite" periods of time, this seemed to set a very worrisome precedent for dealing with people in a free society. At the same time, it makes sense to allow judges to extend the period suspects are detained if evidence is presented to a judge that indicates their release will endanger the public. And most people might have had trouble understanding why the FBI was not allowed to receive information the CIA collects overseas (on the grounds that it would violate our privacy law). Imagine that the CIA intercepts a conversation in a Middle Eastern country that indicates that Osama bin Laden has just given the green light for the next attack, this one with a small nuclear device, to his American associates. It seems difficult to comprehend that this information should be kept from our domestic law enforcement authorities. The Constitution is not a suicide pact.

Immigration rights bring up a complex set of issues that deserve airing well beyond the issues concerning public safety (see chapters 6, 7, and 8 by Mark Krikorian, David Cole, and Douglas Kmiec, respectively). The difficulties start with the observations that everyone who is in the United States (or, for that matter, any place) has some inalienable rights, say, those enumerated in the UN Universal Declaration of Human Rights. At the same time, few disagree that immigrants do not have all the rights of American citizens—for instance, they cannot vote. (In some other countries they are accorded these rights in local elections.) Where to draw the line has been a difficult and highly charged matter. It seems to require especially urgent attention not merely because practically all those who attacked us were foreigners but also because we seem to mix harsh measures (deporting immigrants who committed a minor crime even if married to Americans and if they have American-born children) with very lax ones (often allowing illegal immigrants who have been granted a hearing to roam free until the hearing and not acting when they simply do not show up, in the many thousands). Possible future deliberations have to draw a much sharper line between legal immigrants and illegal "immigrants." The former have come to these shores after being relatively carefully reviewed (including their criminal record), often after having waited for many years for their turn, with the understanding that they will become full-fledged Americans in due process. Illegal "immigrants" are foreigners who first entered the United States by violating the law or who stayed beyond their allotted time, often without any or only minimal preliminary screening, jumping the long queue of their own countrymen and -women, and to whom no promise of citizenship was ever made. Treating immigrants and law-violating aliens quite differently seems to make sense. (It might be said that we need the millions of illegal "immigrants" for the work Americans do not wish to do. In that case, we should increase the level of legal, scrutinized immigration rather than allow those who came here only on a tourist or student visa to make that decision for us.)

The discussion of racial profiling has been especially troubling, starting with the term itself. Many of the groups discussed in this context—Muslim Americans, Arab Americans, and Middle Easterners, for example—do not constitute a race (the U.S. census counts them as whites). Any way one looks at these groups, they are either a religious or an ethnic group but not a race. By referring to the matter at hand as one that concerns racial rather than ethnic profiling, one plays on the strong emotion the abuse of African Americans invokes, which has no equivalent in our history. Next, in the tradition of extreme advocacy, reference is frequently made in this context to the mass detention of Japanese Americans during World War II—warning us that we should not treat our Middle Eastern citizens this way—and in the process disregarding the fact that we have made great progress in this matter, to the point that no one—not even on the extreme right—as much as mentioned anything remotely resembling such acts. It would have been unacceptable even if public authorities merely asked a few questions of the millions of Muslim Americans despite the fact that all the terrorists, as far as we knew in the days following September 11, were members of this group.

However, given that there were strong indications that other hijackings or chemical or biological attacks (using crop dusters) might have been about to strike, it would have been extremely unreasonable not to ask a few extra questions of Middle Eastern young male pilots with recent licenses about to mount long-distance flights. Just think: If this marker had not been used and authorities had to question all young males or even merely all pilots, the screening would have taken a hundred times longer—allowing ample time for the terrorists lying in wait to act. The law has long recognized the reasonable person rule, permitting that which a reasonable person would do. If using the ethnic marker under the said circumstances was unreasonable, it sure is hard to understand what reasonable is. (These are some of the issues that Michael Kinsley and John Derbyshire confront in chapters 9 and 10, respectively.)

Much attention has been paid, as it ought to have been, to the balance between public safety and rights, such as the right to privacy, anonymity, due process, and freedom of movement. Much less attention has been given to military violations of the First Amendment. For decades now, based largely on the way the press helped generate opposition to the war in Vietnam, the armed forces have drawn the conclusion that the military is better off if the public is informed as little as possible about its plans and actions (as longtime journalists Robert Zelnick and Steven Roberts, now both journalism professors, detail in chapters 11 and 12, respectively). There have been some indications that this belief has dictated and will continue to dictate coverage of the war against terrorism. This tough issue deserves more attention. Here too we must find a better point of balance, which most likely requires more access for and disclosure to the media. Many disastrous operations—concocted by planners with little understanding of the cultures and societies involved, trained on computer war games—would gain a healthy reality check if they were dissected by the fourth estate. I am not arguing for disclosing everything. Naming CIA agents who work covertly in other countries is criminal, and I would ban the publication of how to make nuclear weapons in one's basement. But there is much more room for disclosure without violating such taboos.

## THE THREE-LEGGED SOCIETY

Communitarians have long been interested in the proper division of labor, resources, and authority among the government, the private sector, and the community (voluntary associations and religious institutions included). Over the past few years, much has been made about the need to steer more services to the private sector and to communities. Whether we leaned too far in this direction was an issue about which some of us have been concerned, even before the assault on America. Privatization of prisons raised numerous issues, as did the ways we privatized the purchase of plutonium from Russia and, to accommodate business, removed export controls on high-power technologies of great interest to foreign powers.[2] Albert Hunt of the *Wall Street Journal* has some wise words on how we are now turning back to the public sector for guidance in the wake of September 11 (chapter 21).

Essential for public security in this new era will be engaging Americans in their own defense. Indeed, homeland protection is a fine outlet for both the patriotism and the anxiety spawned by the terrorist attacks. If Americans are busy helping to guard our water resources, dams, borders, airports, and other vital public resources and spaces, they will transform their nagging anxieties into socially productive activities. Just as one urges depressed couch potatoes, marooned before their televisions sets, to get out and do something, so we must encourage Americans consumed by fears of terrorists to get off their duffs and actively participate in protecting themselves, their loved ones, and their country. Exactly how Americans should assume this new civic duty is a matter for debate, one to which Senator John McCain, Paul Glastris, and Michael Lind have all made important contributions in their chapters (chapters 16, 17, and 18, respectively).

In addition to security, public health is a communitarian service of the highest order. It concerns itself with those matters that affect all of us rather than just certain individuals. When individual desires conflict with the needs of the community—say, if parents neglect the immunization of their children or if libertarians argue that each person rather than the government should fluoridate their water (even though the public is stuck with many of the costs of dental care)—public health is there to speak for the rest of us. And of course it deals with infectious diseases and the threat of biological warfare. As Alan Kraut, Fitzhugh Mullan, and Richard Riegelman discuss in their "communitarian dialogue" on this subject, the time has come to accord much more standing, resources, and authority to public health (chapter 13).

## HOMELAND SECURITY STARTS OVERSEAS

When all is said and done, there is something profoundly wrong about separating these domestic deliberations from discussions about how we are going to try to prevent terrorism from rising (rather than "hardening" the targets they seek to strike). Here the most telling observation is that free societies rear or sponsor few international terrorists; authoritarian and totalitarian nations are their primary homes. If we try to deal with terrorist attacks mainly by heightening our defenses, we shall need to curb even more of our freedoms of movement, of assembly, and of commerce. Ultimately, we shall turn into a garrison state and still not be safe. Britain enacted all kinds of rights-limiting laws to protect itself from Irish terrorists who shot a missile at the British equivalent of the White House and planted a bomb next to its CIA headquarters. Israelis fear going to malls, bus stops, and movies despite all the measures they have taken. Most important, if we succeed in effectively blocking one form of attack—by putting armed marshals on airlines, for example—we shall shift the terrorists' efforts to other avenues of attack. (This is what happened when we made it more difficult to place car bombs; they took to the air.) The only way to cut off all the heads of the terrorism Hydra is to strike at its heart.

Yet when we consider engaging in any act of war, we must ask, Are our actions morally justified? This raises further questions concerning the nature of the provocation, whether other ways of enhancing our safety have been found to be inadequate, and the specific means of warfare to be employed—for instance, if we shall be forced to harm a large number of civilians. These are issues that have historically been explored in the "just war" tradition. In their open letters on the war on terrorism (chapters 14 and 15), two separate groups of scholars engage many of these questions—and reach very different conclusions.

Clearly, this book is an unconventional collection of material: congressional testimony, summaries of legislation, open letters, and a dialogue, as well as traditional essays. But despite their different formats, when brought together these disparate pieces serve to provide an overview of the main issues that have dominated public debate after September 11— issues that all engage the communitarian concern for achieving a proper balance between civil rights and the common good. As new conflicts (e.g.,

with Iraq) arise and others recede, this communitarian concern will continue to inform public dialogue, although each new challenge will have to be addressed in its own right.[3]

## NOTES

1. Laurie Goodstein, "Falwell's Finger-Pointing Inappropriate, Bush Says," *New York Times,* September 15, 2001, A15.

2. For more documentation on this point, see Amitai Etzioni, *Next: The Road to the Good Society* (New York: Basic Books, 2001), 48–51.

3. For ongoing communitarian analysis of these issues, visit the Communitariann Network's web site (www.gwu.edu/~ccps).

# I

# THE BASICS

# ❶

# A CLEAR AND PRESENT DANGER

## Attorney General John D. Ashcroft

*The following is excerpted from Attorney General Ashcroft's testimony before the House Committee on the Judiciary on September 24, 2001.*

**M**r. Chairman and members of the committee, the American people do not have the luxury of unlimited time in erecting the necessary defenses to future terrorist acts. The danger that darkened the United States of America and the civilized world on September 11 did not pass with the atrocities committed that day. They require that we provide law enforcement with the tools necessary to identify, dismantle, disrupt, and punish terrorist organizations before they strike again.

Terrorism is a clear and present danger to Americans today. Intelligence information available to the FBI indicates a potential for additional terrorist incidents. As a result, the FBI has requested through the national threat warning system that all law enforcement agencies nationwide be on heightened alert.

When we have threat information about a specific target, we share that information with appropriate state and local authorities. We have contacted several city and state officials over the last thirteen days to alert them to potential threats.

We also act on intelligence information to neutralize potential terrorist attacks using specific methods. Yesterday the FBI issued a nationwide alert based on information they received indicating the possibility of attacks using crop-dusting aircraft. The FBI assesses the uses of this type of aircraft to distribute chemical or biological weapons of mass destruction as potential threats to Americans. We have no clear indication of the time or place of any such attack.

The FBI has confirmed that Mohammed Atta, one of the suspected hijackers, was acquiring knowledge of crop-dusting aircraft prior to the attacks on September 11. The search of computers, computer disks, and personal baggage of another individual whom we have in custody revealed a significant amount of information downloaded from the Internet about aerial application of pesticides or crop dusting.

At our request, the Federal Aviation Administration has grounded such aircraft until midnight tonight. In addition to its own preventative measures, the FBI has strongly recommended that state, local, and other federal law enforcement organizations take steps to identify crop-dusting aircraft in their jurisdictions and ensure that they are secured.

I also urge Americans to notify immediately the FBI of any suspicious circumstances that may come to their attention regarding crop-dusting aircraft or any other possible terrorist threat. The FBI Web site is . . . www.ifccfbi.org. Our toll free telephone number is 866-483-5137. . . . The highly coordinated attacks of September 11 make it clear that terrorism is the activity of expertly organized, highly coordinated, and well-financed organizations and networks. These organizations operate across borders to advance their ideological agendas. They benefit from the shelter and protection of like-minded regimes. They are undeterred by the threat of criminal sanctions, and they are willing to sacrifice the lives of their members in order to take the lives of innocent citizens of free nations.

This new terrorist threat to Americans on our soil is a turning point in American history. It's a new challenge for law enforcement. Our fight against terrorism is not merely or primarily a criminal justice endeavor. It is [a] defense of our nation and its citizens. We cannot wait for terrorists to strike to begin investigations and to take action. The death tolls are too high, the consequences too great. We must prevent first—we must prosecute second.

The fight against terrorism is now the highest priority of the Department of Justice. As we do in each and every law enforcement mission we undertake, we are conducting this effort with a total commitment to protect the rights and privacy of all Americans and the constitutional protections we hold dear.

In the past when American law enforcement confronted challenges to our safety and security from espionage, drug trafficking, and organized crime, we have met those challenges in ways that preserve our fundamental freedoms and civil liberties. Today we seek to meet the challenge of terrorism [that is] within our borders and targeted at our friends and neighbors with the same careful regard for the constitutional rights of Americans and respect for all human beings.

Just as American rights and freedoms have been preserved throughout previous law enforcement campaigns, they must be preserved throughout this war on terrorism. This Justice Department will never waver in its defense of the Constitution or relent in our defense of civil rights. The American spirit that rose from the rubble in New York knows no prejudice and defies division by race, ethnicity, or religion. A spirit which binds us and the values that define us will light Americans' path from this darkness.

At the Department of Justice, we are charged with defending Americans' lives and liberties. We are asked to wage war against terrorism within our own borders. Today we seek to enlist your assistance, for we seek new laws against America's enemies, foreign and domestic. As the members of this committee understand, the deficiencies in our current laws on terrorism reflect two facts. First, our laws fail to make defeating terrorism a national priority. Indeed, we have tougher laws against organized crime and drug trafficking than terrorism. Second, technology has dramatically outpaced our statutes.

Law enforcement tools created decades ago were crafted for rotary telephone—not e-mail, the Internet, mobile communications, and voice mail. Every day that passes with outdated statutes and the old rules of engagement—each day that so passes is a day that terrorists have a competitive advantage. Until Congress makes these changes, we are fighting an unnecessarily uphill battle. Members of the committee, I regret to inform you that we are today sending our troops into the modern field of battle with antique weapons. It is not a prescription for victory. The antiterrorism proposals that have been submitted by the administration represent carefully balanced, long-overdue improvements to our capacity to combat terrorism. It is not a wish list; it is a modest set of proposals

—essential proposals focusing on five broad objectives, which I will briefly summarize.

First, law enforcement needs a strengthened and streamlined ability for our intelligence-gathering agencies to gather the information necessary to disrupt, weaken, and eliminate the infrastructure of terrorist organizations. Critically we also need the authority for our law enforcement to share vital information with our national security agencies in order to prevent future terrorist attacks.

Terrorist organizations have increasingly used technology to facilitate their criminal acts and hide their communications from law enforcement. Intelligence-gathering laws that were written for an era of land-line telephone communications are ill-adapted for use in communications over multiple cell phones and computer networks—communications that are also carried by multiple telecommunications providers located in different jurisdictions.

Terrorists are trained to change cell phones frequently, to route e-mail through different Internet computers in order to defeat surveillance. Our proposal creates a more efficient technology-neutral standard for intelligence gathering, ensuring law enforcement's ability to trace the communications of terrorists over cell phones, computer networks, and the new technologies that may be developed in the years ahead. These changes would streamline intelligence-gathering procedures only. We do not seek changes in the underlying protections in the law for the privacy of law-abiding citizens. The information captured by the proposed technology-neutral standard would be limited to the kind of information you might find in a phone bill, such as the phone numbers dialed by a particular telephone. The content of these communications in this setting would remain off limits to monitoring by intelligence authorities, except under the current legal standards where content is available under the law which we now use.

Our proposal would allow a federal court to issue a single order that would apply to all providers in the communications chain, including those outside the region where the court is located. We need speed in identifying and tracking down terrorists. Time is of the essence. The ability of law enforcement to trace communications into jurisdictions without obtaining an additional court order can be the difference between life and death for American citizens. We are not asking the law to expand, just to grow as technology grows. This information has historically been available when criminals used predigital technologies. This same information should be available to law enforcement officials today.

Second, we must make fighting terrorism a national priority in our criminal justice system. In his speech to the Congress, President Bush said that Osama bin Laden's terrorist group, al-Qaeda, is to terror what the mafia is to organized crime. However, our current laws make it easier to prosecute members of organized crime than to crack down on terrorists who can kill thousands of Americans in a single day. The same is true of drug traffickers and individuals involved in espionage. Our laws treat these criminals, and those who aid and abet them, more severely than our laws treat terrorists.

We would make harboring a terrorist a crime. Currently, for instance, harboring persons engaged in espionage is a specific criminal offense, but harboring terrorists is not. Given the wide terrorist network suspected of participating in the September 11 attacks, both in the United States and in other countries, we must punish anyone who harbors a terrorist. Terrorists can run, but they should have no place to hide. Our proposal also increases the penalties for conspiracy to commit terrorist acts to a serious level, as we have done for many drug crimes.

Third, we seek to enhance the authority of the Immigration and Naturalization Service to detain or remove suspected alien terrorists from within our borders. The ability of alien terrorists to move freely across our borders and operate within the United States is critical to their capacity to inflict damage on our citizens and facilities. Under current law, the existing grounds for removal of aliens for terrorism are limited to direct material support of an individual terrorist. We propose to expand these grounds for removal to include material support to terrorist organizations. We propose that any alien that provides material support to an organization that he or she knows or should know is a terrorist organization should be subject to removal from the United States.

Fourth, law enforcement must be able to follow the money in order to identify and neutralize terrorist networks. Sophisticated terrorist operations require substantial financial resources. On Sunday evening, President Bush signed a new executive order under the International Emergency Economic Powers Act, IEEPA, blocking the assets and the transactions of individuals and organizations with terrorist organizations and other business organizations that support terrorism. President Bush's new executive order will allow intelligence, law enforcement, and financial regulatory agencies to follow the money trail to the terrorists and to freeze the money to disrupt their actions. This executive order means that the United States banks that have assets of these groups or individuals must freeze their accounts. And United States citizens or businesses are prohibited from doing businesses with those accounts.

At present, the president's powers are limited to freezing assets and blocking transactions with terrorist organizations. We need the capacity for more than a freeze. We must be able to seize. Doing business with terrorist organizations must be a losing proposition. Terrorist financiers must pay a price for their support of terrorism which kills innocent Americans.

Consistent with the president's action yesterday and his statements this morning, our proposal gives law enforcement the ability to seize the terrorists' assets. Further, criminal liability is imposed on those who knowingly engage in financial transactions or money laundering involving the proceeds of terrorist acts.

Finally, we seek the ability for the president of the United States and the Department of Justice to provide swift emergency relief to the victims of terrorism and their families. Mr. Chairman, I want you to know that the investigation into the acts of September 11 is ongoing, moving aggressively forward. To date the FBI and INS have arrested or detained 352 individuals . . . there are other individuals—392—who remain at large because we think they have . . . information that could be helpful to the investigation.

The investigation has yielded 324 searches, 103 court orders, 3,410 subpoenas, and the potential tips are still coming in to the website and the 1-800 hot line. The web site has received almost 80,000 potential tips, the hot line almost 15,000.

Now it falls to us, in the name of freedom and those who cherish it, to ensure our nation's capacity to defend ourselves from terrorists. Today I urge the Congress, I call upon the Congress to act, to strengthen our ability to fight this evil wherever it exists, and to ensure that the line between the civil and the savage, so brightly drawn on September 11, is never crossed again.

# A VISION FOR UNITING AND STRENGTHENING AMERICA

## Senator Patrick Leahy

*The following is a summary of Senator Leahy's Uniting and Strengthening America (USA) Act, released on September 21, 2001.*

## STRENGTHENING OUR DOMESTIC SECURITY AGAINST TERRORIST ACTS

Authorize the Attorney General to establish an FBI Office for Counterterrorism and Homeland Security headed by a Senate-confirmed Deputy FBI Director to coordinate a National Strategy for Counterterrorism and Homeland Security;

Authorize the Director of OMB, in consultation with the Attorney General and the Assistant to the President for National Security Affairs, to prepare a single National Counterterrorism and Homeland Security Program Budget for submission to Congress;

Establish an FBI Security Officer Career Program;

Establish a Counterterrorism Fund in the Treasury of the United States to reimburse Justice Department components for any costs incurred in connection with providing support to counter, investigate, or prosecute domestic or international terrorism;

Sense of the Congress condemning hate crimes and violence against Arab-Americans, Muslim Americans, and Americans from South Asia.


## UPDATING AND ENHANCING SURVEILLANCE PROCEDURES WITHIN CONSTITUTIONAL BOUNDS

Add to offense predicates for criminal wiretaps: terrorism crimes and felony violations of 18 U.S.C. §1030 (relating to computer fraud and abuse);

Clarify circumstances for sharing of information obtained from criminal wiretaps with intelligence community by amending 18 U.S.C. § 2517(1);

Update of pen register and trap and trace device provisions by allowing nationwide service of orders, clarifying application of such orders to computer and other electronic transmissions, and enhancing judicial review of basis for issuance of order;

Authorize "roving wiretap" under FISA [the Foreign Intelligence Surveillance Act] for surveillance of foreign agents, including suspected international terrorists;

Authorize the FBI Director to expedite employment of translators to support FBI counterterrorism investigations and operations;

Extend FISA electronic surveillance (not search) renewal period from ninety days to one year for non-U.S. persons who are officers or employees of foreign governments;

Increase from seven to fourteen the number of federal judges designated by the Chief Justice to serve on the FISA Court;

Increase and fully fund the FBI's Technical Support Center established in the Anti-Terrorism and Effective Death Penalty Act of 1996.

## STOPPING FINANCIAL SUPPORT FOR TERRORISTS BY STRENGTHENING MONEY LAUNDERING LAWS

Add terrorism, terrorism support, and foreign corruption offenses to offense predicates for money laundering;

Add anti–money laundering measures for United States bank accounts that are used by foreign persons;

Grant United States courts long arm jurisdiction over foreign persons in civil money laundering cases;

Add foreign banks to the definition of financial institutions under the money laundering statutes;

Require the Secretary of the Treasury to issue regulations to ensure that concentration accounts are not used to hide the identity of customers who transfer funds;

Allow the government to charge multiple money laundering transactions in a single count;

Provide for forfeiture of funds deposited in United States interbank accounts through foreign banks;

Allow the Secretary of the Treasury to impose special reporting requirements and other measures for jurisdictions, financial institutions, or international transactions of primary money laundering concern;

Grant financial institutions civil immunity for reporting suspected money laundering activity to the government, and prohibit financial institutions and government officers from disclosing such reports to persons involved in suspicious transactions;

Grant financial institutions civil immunity for disclosing suspicions of criminal wrongdoing in a written employment reference on a current or former employee;

Create penalties for violations of geographic targeting orders and certain record-keeping requirements, and lengthen the effective period of geographic targeting orders;

Sense of the Congress that U.S. should encourage efforts by foreign governments to combat money laundering and official corruption.

## TIGHTENING SECURITY ON THE NORTHERN BORDER

Waive cap on personnel assigned to Immigration and Naturalization Service to address security needs along the Northern Border;

Authorize the tripling of the number of Border Patrol and U.S. Customs Service personnel assigned to each State along the Northern Border;

Allot additional funding for technological improvements and acquire additional equipment to enhance monitoring of cross-border traffic;

Provide the State Department and INS with access to the National Crime Information Center (NCIC) to determine whether visa applicants and applicants for admission to the United States have criminal history records.

## REMOVING OBSTACLES TO INVESTIGATING TERRORISM

Clarify standards of professional conduct that govern attorneys for the Federal Government to ensure that Federal prosecutors and agents can engage in traditional covert activities without running afoul of State bar rules;

Direct the Judicial Conference of the United States to develop uniform national rules of professional conduct to govern areas in which local rules may interfere with effective Federal law enforcement;

Eliminate statute of limitations for certain international terrorism offenses;

Reimburse United States counterterrorism law enforcement and intelligence community personnel for professional liability insurance;

Provide special "danger pay" allowances for FBI agents in hazardous duty locations outside the United States, as is provided for agents of the Drug Enforcement Administration;

Permit the FBI to enter into cooperative projects with foreign countries to improve law enforcement or intelligence operations;

Authorize the Attorney General to offer rewards—payments to individuals who offer information pursuant to a public advertisement—to gather information to combat terrorism and defend the nation against terrorist acts.

## PROTECTING VICTIMS OF TERRORISM AND FAMILIES OF PUBLIC SAFETY OFFICERS

Streamline the Public Safety Officers' Benefits application process for family members of law enforcement officers, firefighters, and emergency personnel who perish or suffer great injury in connection with prevention, investigation, rescue, or recovery efforts related to a terrorist attack;

Authorize the Office for Victims of Crime (OVC) to use up to 50 percent of the amounts remaining in the Crime Victims Fund in FY2002, after regular distributions, for the benefit of the victims of the September 11 attacks, and to replenish the antiterrorism emergency reserve by setting aside up to $50 million;

Give OVC the flexibility to deliver timely and critically-needed assistance to victims of terrorism and mass violence occurring within the United States and otherwise improve the manner in which the Crime Victims Fund is managed and preserved;

Provide enhanced retirement benefits to career law enforcement officers and Federal prosecutors, who may be involved in protecting against terrorist attacks and investigating and prosecuting terrorism cases.

## INCREASING INFORMATION SHARING FOR CRITICAL INFRASTRUCTURE PROTECTION

Expand Department of Justice Regional Information Sharing Systems (RISS) Program to facilitate information sharing among Federal, State, and local law enforcement agencies to investigate and prosecute terrorist conspiracies and activities;

Limit disclosure of critical infrastructure information voluntarily submitted to government agencies under agreement of confidentiality if release would inhibit voluntary provision of such information in the future, and the information aids the government in responding to terrorist threats and fulfilling its national security mission;

Authorize establishment of cybersecurity working groups with Federal employees and outside organizations.

## STRENGTHENING CRIMINAL LAWS AGAINST TERRORISM AND REGULATING BIOLOGICAL WEAPONS

Add certain terrorism offenses to definition of racketeering activity under the RICO [Racketeer-Influenced and Corrupt Organizations] statute;

Prohibit crimes of terrorism and violence directed against mass transportation systems;

Expand criminal penalties for communication of false information concerning biological weapons attacks;

Clarify required reporting of and restriction on possession of biological agents and toxins.

**3**

# WE CAN STRIKE A BALANCE ON CIVIL LIBERTIES

## Laurence H. Tribe

*The following was published in the* Wall Street Journal *on September 27, 2001, between the time that Senator Patrick Leahy and the Bush administration first proposed their antiterrorism legislation and the eventual passage of the USA Patriot Act.*

The monstrous attack on America that took the lives of thousands on September 11, 2001, sent waves of anguish through the nation, setting in motion a response whose outlines we are just beginning to sketch. The way we complete that sketch will determine whether the terrorists will destroy more than lives and towering structures but also the very foundations of our freedom.

To watch Congress take up a complex set of antiterrorism measures with lightning speed, with the usually lumbering Senate passing the whole legislative package in less than thirty minutes, is a refreshing change. But institutional checks against intemperate action are there for a reason. David Hume, in his "Enquiries," said justice must be suspended in times of war.[1] Our Constitution's approach is different, specifying the few limited areas—like the quartering of soldiers in private homes—where a wartime exception is made and treating constitutional principles as otherwise universally applicable. The Constitution is written mostly in measured rather than absolute terms. Witness the ban on "unreasonable" searches and seizures. As Chief Justice William Rehnquist wrote, "The laws will . . . not be silent in time of war, but they will speak with a somewhat different voice."[2] Given the Constitution's flexibility, there can be no excuse for not subjecting all our wartime practices to its scrutiny.

That said, some proposals, being overdue and entirely constitutional responses to technological change, must be enacted promptly. Existing provisions dealing with biological threats have not kept pace with bioterrorism and should be broadened. Cell phones have made wiretap warrants limited to particular phone lines obsolete; wiretap authority applying to a suspect personally, and regardless of the phone he uses, is sensible and constitutional. The same holds for voice-mail messages: If search warrants suffice to seize non-voice-mail messages, they should suffice to seize stored voice mail.

New legislation need not be limited to measures that catch up with technology. Asset forfeiture and other provisions of our antiracketeering laws should be extended to terrorist groups. Terrorist offenses should be subjected to enhanced penalties and denied the shield of statutes of limitations. Congress should add preventive steps providing greater security, including federalizing airport check-ins, more armed federal marshals on airplanes and trains, tightening federal controls on crop dusters and other private aircraft, and enlarging the budget for hiring and training counterterrorism infiltrators fluent in the suspects' languages.

Other proposals should be enacted only after tightening safeguards against abuse. For instance, measures to increase sharing of wiretap and other surveillance information within the intelligence community need controls to prevent a recurrence of the FBI's infamous leaks about Martin Luther King Jr.'s personal life.

But when asked to confer open-ended powers of a sort that governments crave, Congress should put on the brakes. The proposed legislation would, for example, give government sweeping authority to detain, without bail and for an indefinite time, any alien—even one whom there is no basis to deport—citing only "reason to believe" the alien "may" endanger national security. That language is so vague that the existence of judicial review would seem to provide no meaningful safeguard against abuse.

In the same spirit, the act renders deportable any permanent resident alien who ever contributed to a domestic group, including one not then designated a terrorist organization, or any subgroup of which that ever threatened to use a weapon against person or property. That would make resident aliens deportable if they contributed to any of several pro-life organizations, for example. Those provisions endanger freedom of political association and must be narrowed. In at least one crucial respect, the response to the terrorist attack shows a regard for human rights lacking in our response to Pearl Harbor, when we interned Americans of Japanese descent, none of whom had been accused of wrongdoing. How different was the sight of New York Mayor Rudolph Giuliani, soon followed by President Bush, appealing eloquently to Americans not to seek revenge on their fellow citizens who happen to be Muslims.

Grassroots reactions in this instance have lagged behind our political leaders, as vigilante attacks mount and increasing numbers call for ethnic profiling of Arabs and Arab Americans. But there is no sound law enforcement rationale for detention by visual association, for there exists face-recognition software for picking individuals out of crowds far more efficiently and accurately than by the crude use of racial characteristics. Such face-recognition software can and should be deployed—and improved.

There is, of course, a built-in political check when stringent security measures affect us all equally. When Congress weighs the virtues of proposals that would enable the authorities to seize a suspect's voice-mail messages or eavesdrop on e-mail communications, we can be reasonably confident the scales aren't unfairly tipped against individual privacy. But there is danger, far from trivial, that the laws we enact today in response to yesterday's terrorist attack will move the baseline of privacy expectations against which we assess the tools proposed to deal with tomorrow's terrorist attack.

When the Supreme Court held in June 2001 that using infrared technology to measure heat emanating from a home to discover what is inside constitutes a search—and is thus in violation of the Fourth Amendment absent a valid warrant—it circumscribed the "power of technology to shrink the realm of guaranteed privacy."[3] But it also cautioned that, once any technology is "in general public use," its employment by law enforcement agencies to pierce personal privacy might no longer count as a "search" at all. In fact, the public's tolerance for just a bit more government surveillance will grow as authority previously ceded sets an ever-moving precedent. Preventing this phenomenon altogether would be a tall order. At the least, we should limit the momentum of measures adopted in an emergency by making all the powers we grant temporary and designed to lapse unless reenacted by Congress.

It's possible, of course, that what Congress fails to cut back the Supreme Court will strike down. But even if we could count on the Rehnquist Court's misguided belief that it has all the answers, we should act on a theory of "better safe than sorry" and resist the temptation to trust the judiciary to trim the excess. In any event, passing the buck to judges nurtures the undemocratic myth that courts are the sole custodians of constitutional truth.

It is "We the People" in whose name the Constitution was ordained and established; it is we who bear the responsibility to live by it even when the temptation to set it aside seems irresistible. It might be nice if there were a mast to which we could tie ourselves—as Ulysses did to steel himself against the call of the Sirens—to ensure the survival of liberty and equality, but there is none. With or without a Supreme Court steadfastly dedicated to civil rights and liberties, each of us must follow an inner compass that points to the Constitution's true north.

## NOTES

This chapter originally appeared in the *Wall Street Journal*, September 27, 2001, A18.

1. David Hume, *Enquiries concerning Human Understanding and concerning the Principles of Morals*, ed. P. H. Nidditch (Oxford: Clarendon Press, 1975), 187–88.

2. William H. Rehnquist, *All the Laws but One: Civil Liberties in Wartime* (New York: Alfred A. Knopf, 1998), 225.

3. *Kyllo v. United States*, 533 U.S. 27 (2001).

**4**

# ANTITERRORISM TOOLS: A SUMMARY OF THE USA PATRIOT ACT AND THE ORDER ON MILITARY TRIBUNALS

*The following is a summary of the Uniting and Strengthening America by Providing Appropriate Tools Required to Intercept and Obstruct Terrorism Act (USA Patriot Act),[1] passed by Congress on October 25, 2001, and signed into law by President Bush on October 26, and the Department of Defense's Order on Military Tribunals,[2] issued on March 21, 2002.*

## USA PATRIOT ACT

### Enhancing Criminal Investigative Authorities

The USA Patriot Act permits seizure of voice mail pursuant to a search warrant, allows victims of computer trespassing (i.e., hacking) to invite law enforcement to monitor attacks on their computer networks without needing a court order, and allows pen registers and "tap and trace" devices—traditionally used on phones to detect numbers dialed by, and those dialing in to, a target phone—to be used on computer transmissions to obtain "dialing, routing, addressing, and signaling information." Officials can subpoena the addresses and times of e-mail messages sent by terrorism suspects, equating e-mail communications with those made by telephone, for which authorities can already obtain records of numbers called and the duration of calls. However, the law also prohibits investigators from including the content of those electronic communications. Likewise, the act includes Internet sessions in the scope of subpoenas for records of electronic communications but not the content of those sessions. It also allows federal officials to obtain nationwide search warrants for terrorism investigations, including for electronic surveillance.

### Facilitating Intelligence Surveillance Procedures

The act enables law enforcement officials to obtain from the Foreign Surveillance Court (FSC), a special intelligence court, the authority for roving wiretaps on a person suspected of involvement in terrorism so that any telephone used by that person may be monitored. In the past, authorities had to return to the FSC to receive separate authorizations for each phone used by the suspect. Originally, the administration sought the power to use foreign wiretaps that would have been illegal in the United States; the USA Patriot Act denies this request. The administration also wanted to make permanent the newly expanded surveillance powers for tapping telephones and computers; the act includes a sunset provision, which stipulates that these powers will expire in four years, but any information learned from expanded wiretaps in those four years will still be permissible in court cases after that time.

### Lowering the Barriers between Intelligence and Law Enforcement

The act allows intelligence officials and criminal justice officials to share information on investigations, including information obtained through wiretaps and grand-jury investigations. National security investigators will be able to obtain from the FSC the authority to wiretap suspects in terrorism cases if they assert that foreign intelligence is "a significant purpose" of the investigation. Previously, criminal investigations could only provide guidance or direction to intelligence collectors, and vice versa, when foreign intelligence was "the purpose" of an investigation.

## Thwarting Money Laundering

The act allows the government to confiscate the assets of foreign terrorist organizations, the terrorists themselves, and those who aid them. The Treasury Department will be able to require banks to make much greater efforts to determine the sources of large overseas private banking accounts and will also be able to impose sanctions on nations that withhold information from American investigators on depositors. The act also allows the monitoring of *hawalas*, the nearly paperless banks of the Middle East, and bars American banks from doing business with offshore shell banks, which have no connection to any regulated banking industry.

## Addressing Immigration

The USA Patriot Act expands grounds for deeming an alien inadmissible to or deportable from the United States for terrorist activity, provides for the mandatory detention of aliens whom the attorney general or the commissioner of immigration certifies as posing a risk to national security, and facilitates information sharing within the United States and with foreign governments. For the purposes of deportation or denying admission to the United States, the bill also expands the definition of terrorists to include public endorsement of terrorist activity or provision of material support to terrorist organizations. Detained aliens may be held for up to seven days for questioning, after which time they must be released if they are not charged with violations of the criminal or immigration codes. In cases where deportation is determined appropriate but not possible, detention may continue on a review by the attorney general every six months. Originally, the administration sought the power to detain indefinitely and without charges immigrants suspected of involvement in terrorism.

## Strengthening Criminal Laws

The act extends criminal penalties for unauthorized possession of biological agents, toxins, or delivery systems for any purpose besides a "peaceful" one. It adds a list of specified crimes to the definition of a "federal crime of terrorism," increases penalties and statutes of limitations on terrorist crimes, strengthens the penalties for hiding terrorists, and defines cyberterrorist threats. According to the new law, committing an act of terrorism against a mass transit system becomes a federal crime, and parties to a terrorist conspiracy can be punished as severely as the perpetrators.

## DEPARTMENT OF DEFENSE
## ORDER ON MILITARY COMMISSIONS

A military commission is a wartime, military tribunal traditionally used to try violations of the laws of war. Under the President's Military Order of November 13, 2001, those tried by military commission may include:
Members of al-Qaeda;
People involved in acts of international terrorism against the United States;
People who knowingly harbored such terrorists.

### Commission Membership and Selection

Commissions will consist of at least three but no more than seven members, with one or two alternates.

The secretary of defense may appoint members and other commission personnel or select an appointing authority to choose commission personnel.

Commission members are officers in the U.S. armed forces, including reserve personnel, National Guard members, and retired personnel recalled to active duty.

A presiding officer will be chosen from among the commission members to preside over commission proceedings. The presiding officer will be a judge advocate of any branch of the armed forces.
The presiding officer has the authority to admit or exclude evidence.
The presiding officer also has the authority to close proceedings to protect classified information or to protect the safety of defendants, witnesses, and commission members.

## A Full and Fair Trial

Military defense counsel will be provided for the accused. In addition, the accused may choose their own counsel: another military officer who is a judge advocate of the U.S. armed forces or a civilian attorney. Civilian attorneys may be prequalified as members of a pool of available attorneys for the defense.

The defendant and counsel will be able to see copies of the charges in their native language in advance of the trial.

The accused is presumed innocent until proven guilty.

The accused may be found guilty only when commission members are convinced of guilt beyond a reasonable doubt.

The accused may refuse to testify during trial.

The accused will be able to obtain witnesses and documents to use in his defense.

The accused may not be tried twice before a military commission for the same offense.

The accused may enter into a plea agreement.

## Trial Format

Trial proceedings will be open unless otherwise determined by the presiding officer. The presiding officer may also allow attendance by the public and press. Photography, video and audio recording, and broadcasting will be prohibited.

A trial may be closed to protect:
  Classified or sensitive information;
  The physical safety of participants;
  Intelligence or law enforcement sources, methods, and activities;
  National security interests.

Commissions will be impartial.

Evidence, including previous trial testimony and written statements, will be admissible if it would have probative value to a reasonable person.

Witnesses will testify under oath and will be subject to direct and cross-examination.

For witness safety, some testimony may be accepted by phone, through the use of pseudonyms, or during closed proceedings.

Commission members will deliberate and vote on findings of guilt, innocence, and sentencing in closed conference.

A conviction requires a vote of two-thirds of the commission.

A death sentence requires a unanimous vote.

Sentences may also include life imprisonment or a lesser term, fines and restitution, or any other punishment deemed appropriate.

A three-member review panel, appointed by the secretary of defense, will review trial findings within thirty days and either provide a recommendation to the secretary of defense or return the case for further proceedings. The panel will include three military officers but may also include civilians temporarily commissioned as military officers.

Findings and sentences are not final until approved by the president or secretary of defense, but findings of "not guilty" cannot be changed.

The procedures may be amended by the secretary of defense to accommodate changed circumstances.


## NOTES

1. Sources: Suzanne Spaulding, "The New Antiterrorism Laws: Finding the Balance," *National Strategy Forum Review* 11, no. 2 (winter 2001): 8–10; Adam Clymer, "Antiterrorism Bill Passes: U.S. Gets Expanded Powers," *New York Times,* October 26, 2001, A1.

2. Department of Defense Fact Sheet on Military Commissions, issued March 21, 2002. The information presented here, while deemed reliable, does not constitute a definitive statement of the procedures applicable to military commissions established under the President's Military Order of November 13, 2001 (available at www.defenselink.mil/news/Mar2002/d20020321fact.pdf; accessed October 6, 2002).

## 5

# THE TRUTH ABOUT OUR LIBERTIES

## Richard A. Posner

In the wake of the September 11 terrorist attacks have come many proposals for tightening security; some measures to that end have already been taken. Civil libertarians are troubled. They fear that concerns about national security will lead to an erosion of civil liberties. They offer historical examples of supposed overreactions to threats to national security. They treat our existing civil liberties—freedom of the press, protections of privacy and of the rights of criminal suspects, and the rest—as sacrosanct, insisting that the battle against international terrorism accommodate itself to them.

I consider this a profoundly mistaken approach to the question of balancing liberty and security. The basic mistake is the prioritizing of liberty. It is a mistake about law and a mistake about history. Let me begin with law. What we take to be our civil liberties—for example, immunity from arrest except upon probable cause to believe we've committed a crime and from prosecution for violating a criminal statute enacted after we committed the act that violates it—were made legal rights by the Constitution and other enactments. The other enactments can be changed relatively easily, by amendatory legislation. Amending the Constitution is much more difficult. In recognition of this, the framers left most of the constitutional provisions that confer rights pretty vague. The courts have made them definite.

Concretely, the scope of these rights has been determined, through an interaction of constitutional text and subsequent judicial interpretation, by a weighing of competing interests. I'll call them the public-safety interest and the liberty interest. Neither, in my view, has priority. They are both important, and their relative importance changes from time to time and from situation to situation. The safer the nation feels, the more weight judges will be willing to give to the liberty interest. The greater the threat that an activity poses to the nation's safety, the stronger will the grounds seem for seeking to repress that activity even at some cost to liberty. This fluid approach is only common sense.

If it is true, therefore, that the events of September 11 have revealed the United States to be in much greater jeopardy from international terrorism than had previously been believed—have revealed it to be threatened by a diffuse, shadowy enemy that must be fought with police measures as well as military force—it stands to reason that our civil liberties will be curtailed. They should be curtailed, to the extent that the benefits in greater security outweigh the costs in reduced liberty. All that can reasonably be asked of the responsible legislative and judicial officials is that they weigh the costs as carefully as the benefits.

It will be argued that the lesson of history is that officials habitually exaggerate dangers to the nation's security. But the lesson of history is the opposite. It is because officials have repeatedly and disastrously underestimated these dangers that our history is as violent as it is. Consider such underestimated dangers as that of secession, which led to the Civil War; of a Japanese attack on the United States, which led to the disaster at Pearl Harbor; of Soviet espionage in the 1940s, which accelerated the Soviet Union's acquisition of nuclear weapons and emboldened Stalin to encourage North Korea's invasion of South Korea; of the installation of Soviet missiles in Cuba, which precipitated the Cuban missile crisis; of political assassinations and outbreaks of urban violence in the 1960s; of the Tet Offensive of 1968; of the Iranian revolution of 1979 and the subsequent taking of American diplomats as hostages; and, for that matter, of the events of September 11.

It is true that when we are surprised and hurt, we tend to overreact—but only with the benefit of hindsight can a reaction be separated into its proper and excess layers. In hindsight we know that interning Japanese Americans did not shorten World War II. But was this known at the time? If not, shouldn't the Army have erred on the side of caution, as it did? Even today we cannot say with any assurance that Abraham Lincoln was wrong to suspend habeas corpus during the Civil War, as he did on several occasions, even though the Constitution is clear that only Congress can suspend this right. (Another of Lincoln's wartime measures, the Emancipation Proclamation, may also have been unconstitutional.) But Lincoln would have been wrong to cancel the 1864 presidential election, as some urged: By November 1864, the North was close to victory, and canceling the election would have created a more dangerous precedent than the wartime suspension of habeas corpus. This last example shows that civil liberties remain part of the balance even in the most dangerous of times and even though their relative weight must then be less.

Lincoln's unconstitutional acts during the Civil War show that even legality must sometimes be sacrificed for other values. We are a nation under law, but first we are a nation. I want to emphasize something else, however: the malleability of law, its pragmatic rather than dogmatic character. The law is not absolute, and the slogan *"Fiat iustitia rat caelum"* (Let justice be done though the heavens fall) is dangerous nonsense. The law is a human creation rather than a divine gift, a tool of government rather than a mandarin mystery. It is an instrument for promoting social welfare, and as the conditions essential to that welfare change, so must it change.

Civil libertarians today are missing something else—the opportunity to challenge other public-safety concerns that impair civil liberties. I have particularly in mind the war on drugs. The sale of illegal drugs is a "victimless" crime in the special but important sense that it is a consensual activity. Usually there is no complaining witness, so in order to bring the criminals to justice, the police have to rely heavily on paid informants (often highly paid and often highly unsavory), undercover agents, wiretaps and other forms of electronic surveillance, elaborate sting operations, the infiltration of suspect organizations, random searches, the monitoring of airports and highways, the "profiling" of likely suspects on the basis of ethnic or racial identity or national origin, compulsory drug tests, and other intrusive methods that put pressure on civil liberties.

The war on drugs has been a big flop; moreover, in light of what September 11 has taught us about the gravity of the terrorist threat to the

United States, it becomes hard to take entirely seriously the threat to the nation that drug use is said to pose. Perhaps it is time to redirect law enforcement resources from the investigation and apprehension of drug dealers to the investigation and apprehension of international terrorists. By doing so we may be able to minimize the net decrease in our civil liberties that the events of September 11 have made inevitable.

# II

# THE SPECIFICS

# Immigration

# 6

# A PRIVILEGE OR A RIGHT?

## Mark Krikorian

Is immigration to the United States a privilege or a right? This is the question we need to address in considering the USA Patriot Act, passed by Congress and signed into law by the president in the wake of the September 11 atrocities. The act gives the Justice Department more flexibility in detaining foreign citizens suspected of involvement with terrorism and facilitates their deportation. Specifically, the USA Patriot Act allows the commissioner of the Immigration and Naturalization Service (INS), in consultation with the attorney general, to recommend the detention of any noncitizen if there is reason to believe the alien poses a risk to national security.

The usual critics have made the usual objections. On the left, the American Civil Liberties Union said the Patriot Act "degrades our system of justice,"[1] while the head of the American Immigration Lawyers Association said the immigration provisions "trample on the Constitution."[2] On the right, the *Wall Street Journal* raised the specter of immigrants being "deported on the flimsiest of pretexts" by the "epic ineptitude" of the INS.[3]

But limiting the number and nature of appeals available to guests whom we want to send home is entirely within our power as a nation. There is no entitlement for foreign citizens to enter or to remain in the United States. In fact, at a time when many are suggesting curbs on the civil liberties of

Americans, it would seem only prudent to first look at measures that do not impact the rights of Americans at all but instead merely change the terms under which we allow guests from overseas to remain here.

Until someone from overseas embraces America by becoming a citizen, he remains here at our discretion. He is protected by the criminal law, he may file civil lawsuits, he may buy and sell property—but his continued residence in the United States depends on the wishes of the American people, expressed through their elected representatives.

Ordinarily, we should welcome whichever legal immigrants and visitors we decide to admit. And, in fact, we take in close to a million legal immigrants per year, plus tens of millions of visitors. What's more, it's much easier for immigrants to become citizens in our country than in virtually any other—last year alone, almost 900,000 foreigners became Americans.

But in a time of national emergency, extraordinary measures may be appropriate. And the focus on immigration issues in the quest for homeland security is not some opportunistic attempt to achieve extraneous political ends under the cover of war. All nineteen hijackers were, after all, foreign citizens, as are many, perhaps most, of those detained as possible accomplices or for suspected involvement in another terrorist plot. This was also the case with the conspirators in the first World Trade Center attack, which resulted in incomplete reforms passed by Congress in 1996.

It would be unfortunate if, in our effort to prevent another 3,000 American deaths—or 30,000 or 300,000—we were inadvertently to deport some foreign citizens who pose no threat to us. But their presence here is a privilege we grant, not a right they have exercised, and we may withdraw that privilege for any reason.

## NOTES

This chapter originally appeared in *The Responsive Community* 12, no. 1 (winter 2001–2): 46–47.

1. American Civil Liberties Union, "From Secret Evidence to No Evidence" (available at www.aclu.org/safeandfree/facts-secret.html; accessed October 14, 2002).

2. Lynda Guydon Taylor, "Organizations Disagree about Immigration Policy after Attack on the Nation," *Pittsburgh Post-Gazette*, September 30, 2001, W3.

3. "Taking Liberties," *Wall Street Journal*, September 25, 2001, A18.

**7**

# LET'S FIGHT TERRORISM, NOT THE CONSTITUTION

## David Cole

The terrorist attacks of September 11 have shocked and stunned us all and have quite properly spurred renewed consideration of our capability to forestall future attacks. Yet in doing so, we must not rashly trample on the very freedoms that we are fighting for. Nothing tests our commitment to principle like fear and terror. But precisely because the terrorists violated every principle of civilized society and human dignity, we must remain true to our principles as we fashion a response.

Three principles in particular should guide our response to the threat of terrorism. First, we should not overreact in a time of fear, a mistake we have made all too often in the past. Second, we should not sacrifice the bedrock foundations of our constitutional democracy—political freedom and equal treatment—absent a compelling showing of need and adoption of narrowly tailored means. And third, in balancing liberty and security, we should not succumb to the temptation to trade a vulnerable minority's liberties, namely, the liberties of immigrants in general or Arab and Muslim immigrants in particular, for the security of the rest of us.

Unfortunately, the USA Patriot Act, our government's first legislative attempt to respond to the threats posed by September 11, violates all three of these principles. It overreacts in just the way that we have so often overreacted in the past: by substituting guilt by association for targeted measures directed at guilty conduct. It violates core constitutional principles, rendering immigrants deportable for their political associations, excludable for pure speech, and detainable on the attorney general's say-so. And by reserving its harshest measures for immigrants—in the immediately foreseeable future, Arab and Muslim immigrants—it sacrifices commitments to equality by trading a minority group's liberty for the majority's security. In addition to being unprincipled, our response will in all likelihood be ineffective. Painting with a broad brush is not a good law enforcement tool. It wastes resources on innocents, alienates the very communities we need to be working with, and makes it all the more difficult to distinguish the true threat from the innocent bystander.

The Patriot Act's principal flaws are as follows: (1) It imposes guilt by association on immigrants, resurrecting a long-abandoned philosophy of the McCarthy era; (2) it authorizes executive detention on mere suspicion that an immigrant has at some point engaged in a violent crime or provided humanitarian aid to a proscribed organization; and (3) it resurrects ideological exclusion, denying admission to aliens for pure speech, resurrecting yet another long-interred relic of the McCarthy era.

## A HISTORY OF MISTAKES

Before turning to the specifics of the Patriot Act, it is worth reviewing a little history and assessing what powers government already had in the fight against terrorism before September 11. Both assessments are critical to asking whether our immediate reactions to the events of September 11 were measured and likely to be effective.

This is not the first time we have responded to fear by targeting immigrants and treating them as suspect because of their group identities rather than their individual conduct. In World War I, we imprisoned "enemy aliens" for their national identity and dissidents for merely speaking out against the war. In the winter of 1919–1920, the federal government responded to a series of politically motivated bombings, including one of Attorney General A. Mitchell Palmer's home in Washington, D.C., by rounding up 6,000 to 10,000 suspected immigrants in thirty-three cities across the country—not for their part in the bombings but for their political affiliations. They were detained in overcrowded "bull pens" and coerced into signing confessions. Many of those arrested turned out to be citizens. In the end, 556 were deported, but for their political affiliations, not for their part in the bombings.

In World War II, we interned 110,000 persons, over two-thirds of whom were citizens of the United States, not because of individualized determinations that they posed a threat to national security or the war effort but solely for their Japanese ancestry. And in the fight against Communism, which reached its height in the McCarthy era, we made it a crime even to be a member of the Communist Party and passed the McCarran–Walter Act, which authorized the government to keep out and expel noncitizens who advocated Communism or other proscribed ideas or who belonged to groups advocating those ideas. Under the McCarran–Walter Act, which remained a part of our law until 1990, the United States denied visas to, among others, writers Gabriel García Márquez and Carlos Fuentes and to Nino Pasti, former deputy commander of NATO, because he was going to speak against the deployment of nuclear cruise missiles.

All these past responses are now seen as mistakes. Yet while today's response does not yet match these historical overreactions, it is characterized by many of the same mistakes of principle—namely, targeting vulnerable groups not for illegal conduct but because of their group identity or political affiliation.

In considering whether the new laws directed at immigrants are necessary, it is also important to know what authority the government had prior to September 11 to deny admission to, detain, and deport aliens engaged in terrorist activity. Before the Patriot Act, the government could detain without bond any alien with any visa violation if it had reason to believe that he posed a threat to national security or a risk of flight. It could deny admission to mere members of terrorist groups, and it could deport any alien who had in any way engaged in, furthered, supported, or facilitated terrorist activity, expansively defined to include virtually any use or threat to use a firearm with intent to endanger person or property. Moreover, the Immigration and Naturalization Service (INS) maintained that it had the power to expel, detain, and deport aliens using secret evidence that the alien had no chance to confront or rebut.

The extent of these preexisting powers is illustrated by the unprecedented incarceration of between 1,500 and 2,000 persons in connection with the investigation of the September 11 attacks. As of December 2002, the identity of the vast majority of these detainees was still a secret, as was even the total number detained. (The government stopped issuing a daily tally in early November 2001, when the number was 1,182.) The bulk of the detainees were held on immigration charges, and all the immigration detainees were tried in proceedings entirely closed to the public, a practice that three federal courts have declared unconstitutional. In October 2002, one court upheld the constitutionality of the closed hearings, and the matter is likely to be resolved in the Supreme Court. As of October 2002, not one person arrested since September 11 had been charged with any involvement in the attacks under investigation. The only person so charged was Zaccarias Moussaoui, and he was arrested before September 11. Most of the detainees have been affirmatively "cleared" by the FBI of any involvement in terrorism. And most important for purposes of assessing the need for new powers, the government carried out this unprecedented program of secret mass detentions without even relying on the Patriot Act.

## GUILT BY ASSOCIATION

The single most problematic feature of the Patriot Act is its adoption of the philosophy of guilt by association, which the Supreme Court has condemned as "alien to the traditions of a free society and the First Amendment itself." Under prior law, aliens were deportable for engaging in or supporting terrorist *activity*. The Patriot Act makes aliens deportable for wholly innocent *associations* with a "terrorist organization," regardless of any nexus between the alien's support and any act of violence, much less terrorism. And because the Patriot Act defines "terrorist activity" to include virtually any use or threat to use violence and defines a "terrorist organization" as any group that has used or threatened to use violence, the proscription on political association potentially encompasses every organization that has ever been involved in a civil war or a crime of violence, from a pro-life group that once threatened workers at an abortion clinic to the African National Congress (ANC), the Irish Republican Army (IRA), or the Northern Alliance in Afghanistan.

The law contains no requirement that the alien's support have any connection whatsoever to a designated organization's terrorist activity. Thus, an alien who sent coloring books to a day care center run by an organization that was ever involved in armed struggle would be deportable as a terrorist, even if she could show that the coloring books were used only by three-year-olds. Indeed, the law apparently extends even to those who seek to support a group in the interest of *countering* terrorism. Thus, an immigrant who offered his services in peace negotiating to the Real IRA in the hope of furthering the peace process in Great Britain and fore-stalling further violence could be deported as a terrorist.

Guilt by association, the Supreme Court has ruled, violates the First and the Fifth Amendments. It violates the First Amendment because people have a right to associate with groups that have lawful and unlaw-ful ends, so long as they do not further the group's illegal ends. And it violates the Fifth Amendment because "in our jurisprudence guilt is personal." To hold an alien responsible for the military acts of the ANC, for example, because he offered a donation to the ANC's peaceful anti-apartheid efforts, or for providing peace-negotiating training to the Real IRA, violates that principle. Without some connection between the alien's support and terrorist activity, the Constitution is violated.

Some suggest that the threat from terrorist organizations abroad re-quires some compromise on the principle prohibiting guilt by associa-tion. But this principle was developed in connection with measures directed at the Communist Party, an organization that Congress found to be, and the Supreme Court accepted as, a foreign-dominated organ-ization that used sabotage and terrorism for the purpose of overthrow-ing the United States by force and violence. Others argue that because money is fungible, even support of lawful activities may free up re-sources that can then be devoted to terrorism. But, of course, the same argument could have been made of the Communist Party or indeed any organization that engages in legal as well as illegal activity. Yet surely it cannot be the case that Congress could have simply reenacted all the anti-Communist laws struck down on guilt by association grounds sim-ply by rewriting them to hinge their penalties on the payment of dues to the Communist Party instead of membership in that party.

## DETENTION VERSUS DUE PROCESS

The Patriot Act also authorizes the INS to detain, potentially indefinitely, any alien certified by the attorney general as a "suspected terrorist."

While "suspected terrorists" sounds like a class that ought to be locked up, the law defines the class so broadly that it includes virtually every immigrant who has been involved in a barroom brawl or domestic dispute, as well as aliens who have never committed an act of violence in their life, and whose only "crime" is to have provided humanitarian aid to an organization disfavored by the government. And the act provides that such persons may be detained indefinitely even if they are *granted* relief from removal—and therefore have a legal right to remain here.

This provision raises several constitutional concerns. First, it mandates preventive detention of persons *who pose no threat to national security or risk of flight.* The Supreme Court has upheld preventive detention of accused criminals and aliens in deportation proceedings, but only where the government demonstrates a specific need for the detention—by showing that the individual poses a danger to others or a risk of flight. In doing away with that minimal requirement, the legislation vests the attorney general with unprecedented and unconstitutional authority.

Second, the law allows the INS to detain aliens *indefinitely, even where they have prevailed in their removal proceedings.* This, too, is patently unconstitutional. Once an alien has prevailed in his removal proceeding and has been granted relief from removal, he has a legal right to remain here. There is no longer a legitimate immigration reason to detain such a person because immigration detention is permissible only as an aid to removing a person from the country. Yet the act provides that even aliens *granted* relief from removal may still be detained. This is akin to detaining a prisoner even after he has received a pardon. Once an alien has prevailed in his immigration proceeding, the INS has no legitimate basis for detaining the individual.

Third, and most important, it is critical to the constitutionality of any executive detention provision that the person detained have a meaningful opportunity to contest his detention both administratively and in court. The bill affords an alien no opportunity to make a case that he should not be detained within the administrative process. It relegates him to the filing of a habeas corpus petition. But due process requires that the agency depriving a person of his liberty afford him a meaningful opportunity to be heard, and the fact that one can sue the agency afterward is not generally sufficient.

Finally, the Patriot Act permits detention of certified aliens for up to seven days without the filing of any charges. The Supreme Court has ruled that individuals arrested in the criminal setting must be brought before a judge for a probable cause hearing within forty-eight hours except in the most extraordinary circumstances. This law extends blanket authority to detain an alien for seven days on mere certification that he or she was at one time involved in a barroom brawl. Such overbroad authority clearly does not meet the Supreme Court's requirement that any preventive detention authority be accompanied by heightened procedural protections and narrowly drawn laws.

## IDEOLOGICAL EXCLUSION

The Patriot Act also revives ideological exclusion, denying entry to aliens for pure speech. It excludes aliens who "endorse or espouse terrorist activity" or who "persuade others to support terrorist activity or a terrorist organization" in ways that the secretary of state determines undermine U.S. efforts to combat terrorism. It also excludes aliens who are representatives of groups that "endorse acts of terrorist activity" in ways that similarly undermine U.S. efforts to combat terrorism.

Excluding people for their ideas and associations is flatly contrary to the spirit of freedom for which the United States stands. Moreover, such exclusions have a negative impact on free debate within the United States by denying those who live here access to those who might dissent from government policies. It was for that reason that Congress repealed all such "ideological exclusion" grounds in 1990 after years of embarrassing visa denials for political reasons. We are a strong enough country, and our resolve against terrorism is strong enough, to make such censorship wholly unnecessary.

## CONCLUSION

We must respond to terrorism, but we must also ensure that our responses are measured and balanced. Is it measured to make deportable anyone who provides humanitarian aid to any organization engaged in a civil war? Is it measured to label domestic disputes or barroom fights with weapons acts of terrorism? Is it measured to subject anyone who might engage in such activity to mandatory detention without any procedural protections and without any showing that he poses any current danger? Is it measured to restore exclusion for pure ideas?

The overbreadth of the Patriot Act reflects the overreaction that we have often indulged in when threatened and raises serious constitutional concerns even if it were shown that such measures would make us more secure. But there is also reason to doubt that the expansive authorities that the act grants will in fact make us safer. By penalizing even wholly lawful, nonviolent, and counterterrorist associational activity, we are likely to waste valuable resources tracking innocent political activity, drive other activity underground, encourage extremists, and make the communities that will inevitably be targeted by such broad-brush measures far less likely to cooperate with law enforcement. As Justice Louis Brandeis wrote nearly seventy-five years ago, the framers of our Constitution knew "that fear breeds repression; that repression breeds hate; and that hate menaces stable government."[1] In other words, freedom and security need not necessarily be traded off against one another; maintaining our freedoms is itself critical to maintaining our security.

The immigration provisions of the Patriot Act fail to live up to the very commitments to freedom that the president has said that we are fighting for. As the Supreme Court wrote in 1967, declaring invalid an anti-Communist law, "It would indeed be ironic if, in the name of national defense, we would sanction the subversion of one of those liberties—the freedom of association—which makes the defense of the Nation worthwhile."[2]

## NOTES

An earlier version of this chapter appeared in *The Responsive Community* 12, no. 1 (winter 2001–2): 48–55.

1. *Whitney v. California*, 274 U.S. 357 (1927).
2. *United States v. Rubel*, 389 U.S. 258 (1967).

## 8

# CONFUSING FREEDOM WITH LICENSE—LICENSES TERRORISM, NOT FREEDOM

## Douglas W. Kmiec

The events of September 11 remain ever present in the minds of American citizens. For thousands of families, a husband or wife or child will never return home because of what happened that day. The diabolical events of that morning will be forever etched in our consciousness. And yet, along with those mental pictures, it is important to grasp fully what happened: It wasn't a political rally, it wasn't a nonviolent speech protest, it wasn't an example of urban street crime, it wasn't even an attack by another sovereign state or nation. It was the deliberate murder of innocent men and women, not for a high political purpose or cause— or even a base one—but simply the random manifestation of hate intended to spread panic and fracture the civil order and continuation of American society.

As grievously wounded as we may be, American society and its principled understanding of freedom *with* responsibility does not fracture or panic that easily. But it does expect that justice will be done. It earnestly desires, along with our president, to see those who so mercilessly took sacred human life to be held accountable—not in a local criminal court but by the able men and women of the military and our law enforcement communities, working together either to eliminate on a field of battle these "enemies of mankind," as Blackstone called them, or to apprehend

and punish them—presumably before the bar of a properly convened
military tribunal, like those employed against Nazi saboteurs in World
War II.

In considering the USA Patriot Act, it is useful to remember that our
founders' conception of freedom was not a freedom to do anything or
associate for any purpose but to do those things that do not harm others
and that, it was hoped, would advance the common good. Freedom separated from this truth is not freedom at all but license. *Congress can no
longer afford, if it ever could, to confuse freedom and license because
doing so licenses terrorism, not freedom.* Those who have voiced opposition to the Patriot Act seem to have either a more extreme view of
freedom, a less sober view of the threats we face, or both.

With due respect, such unrefined autonomy or complacency hides a
basic confusion or underappreciation for the war against terrorism that
now must be fought. The objectors think of the mass destruction of the
World Trade Center and the Pentagon as the equivalent of murder, kid-
naping, or bank robbery. They think the point is a criminal trial; it is
not—it is the elimination of terrorism.

The primary authority for dealing with the terrorist threat resides both
in the president, as commander in chief, and in Congress, as the architect
of various specific legal authorities under the Constitution, to meet that
threat. The president has courageously told the nations of the world
that all are either for the United States in this or with the terrorists. There
is no middle ground. Similarly, Congress, by joint resolution, has given
President Bush authority to act against not only those wealthy and bloody
hands that orchestrated the events of September 11 but also all coopera-
tors in those cowardly actions or "any future act" of international terrorism. However, to ensure successful application of our military might,
Congress needed to equip our law enforcement and intelligence communities with adequate and constitutional legal authority to address a war
crime on a scale that previously was not seen in this generation or seen
ever in peacetime.

The Patriot Act supplied the necessary authority and direction. The act
gives due regard to the necessary balance between the civil liberties enjoyed by our citizens under the Constitution and the law enforcement authority needed. In particular, the act advances two fundamental
purposes: to subject terrorism to at least the same rigorous treatment as

organized crime and prosecution of the drug trade and to supply up-to-date law enforcement capabilities that address the technology of the day, which no longer observes some of the lines previously drawn under existing law. Terrorists don't stay in one place using only land-line telephones and postcards, and it is folly to have a legal investigation authority that still assumes that.

While the Patriot Act's provisions are a bit arcane and complex, they incorporate the recommendations of virtually every commission in the last decade to study terrorism. Specifically, with respect to conducting intelligence gathering against a foreign power or their agents, the act ensures that the insights of the specialized foreign intelligence court are available to superintend the investigative process. There is no reason to deny the Justice Department this authority even if a given investigation has a significant criminal purpose as well. So, too, information gathered on the criminal justice side of an investigation or through a grand jury should be made available to those tasked with the difficult worldwide manhunt of shadowy and elusive terrorist cells. Such are matters of prudent legal reform and just plain common sense.

## WIDENING THE NET

Turning to the immigration provisions, the broadened definition of "terrorist" is necessary to meet the current dangers we now face. Under past law, an alien was inadmissible and deportable for, among other reasons, engaging in a terrorist activity employing "explosives or firearms." The Patriot Act adds the words "or other weapon or dangerous device" to the applicable section of the U.S. Code.

Professor David Cole objects, arguing that expanding the term to include a residual category of other weapons trivializes terrorism. With due respect, this is not constitutional law but opinion—and not likely one shared by the families of the innocent men and women who were killed with a "box cutter" en route to crashing into the World Trade Center or the Pentagon or in rural Pennsylvania. Perhaps, prior to September 11, we could be lulled into the notion that not even terrorists would conceive of using innocent human beings as a weapon against other innocent human beings on our own soil, but sadly that is no longer our reality. Hypothetical objections that the statute might be contorted to apply to a barroom brawl or a domestic dispute are, in my judgment and the present context, too facetious to be credited as a legal objection.

Similarly, opponents of the new law expressed a concern that aliens who associate with terrorist organizations may be deported even when they supposedly kept their association to the nonterrorist functions of the organization. Yet this objection, too, seems overstated. The Patriot Act does not punish those who innocently may support a front organization. Moreover, the act even allows for giving support to an individual who had previously committed a terrorist act if the alien establishes that the individual had renounced his terrorist activity before the alien provided support.

Reality tells us that terrorists unfortunately gain financial and other support hiding behind the facade of charity. Those opposing this new immigration authority seem undisturbed by this. That is again a policy choice; it is not a constitutional one. A statute like the present one, aimed at supplying a general prohibition against an alien contributing funds or other material support to a terrorist organization (as designated under current law by the secretary of state) or to any nondesignated organization that the alien "knows or reasonably should know" furthers terrorist activity, does not violate the Constitution. Some civil libertarians have supported their opposition to this provision by loosely referencing older cases that wrongfully assigned criminal guilt to U.S. citizens for associating with the domestic cause of civil rights in the 1950s and 1960s; such analogies are simply inappropriate. Surely it is possible to draw distinction between nonviolent associations of American citizens, which are entitled to full First Amendment protection, and the fanatical planning of widespread mass destruction against innocents by noncitizens, which clearly is not.

## CONSIDERING INTENT

Still unpersuaded and want the fine print? Well, here it is: "Engaging in terrorist activity" means committing a terrorist act or otherwise committing an act that "the actor knows, or reasonably should know, affords material support . . . [to any organization that the actor knows, or reasonably should know, is a terrorist organization, or] to any individual whom the actor knows, or reasonably should know, has committed or plans to commit any terrorist activity."[1] The specific intent requirements are not only explicit but multiple. This is not, as the objectors claim, "guilt by association" but rather guilt for associating with terrorists for terrorism purposes.

Critics of the Patriot Act have claimed that the First and Fifth Amendments apply without distinction to citizens and aliens residing in the United States. However, this cannot be said without qualification. American citizens enjoy certain privileges and immunities within our constitutional structure that noncitizens do not. Americans, for example, travel freely in and out of our sovereign borders. That same freedom is obviously not afforded noncitizens. With regard to exclusion of immigrants, U.S. authority is plenary, and such authority may be exercised by Congress to prohibit entry altogether. The Court has long held that "whatever the procedure authorized by Congress is, it is due process as far as an alien denied entry is concerned."

Terrorists or those seeking association with them clearly can be excluded from our nation without offending the First Amendment or any other provision of the Constitution. While additional rights do attend an immigrant granted admission, such rights are not necessarily on par with those of citizens. In *U.S. v. Verdugo-Urquidez*, for example, the Court opined that "[our] cases . . . establish only that aliens receive constitutional protections when they have come within the territory of the United States and developed substantial connections with this country."[2] Lower courts have thus upheld the deportation of an alien who associated with groups assisting Nazi persecution, even without proof that the alien himself engaged in the act of persecution.

More problematic is the question of how long those aliens subject to removal who also pose a terrorist threat can be detained by the attorney general. The detention provision was the subject of much debate. The Patriot Act ultimately provided that "the Attorney General *may* certify [for detention] an alien he has reason to believe may commit, further, or facilitate [terrorist] acts . . . or engage in any other activity that endangers the national security of the United States"[3] (emphasis added). This is authority that is reminiscent of that exercised by the United Kingdom against the Irish Republican Army (IRA). In that context in the 1970s, the British secretary of state could issue a detention order against those attempting or carrying out or organizing for the purpose of terrorist activity. In *The Republic of Ireland v. The United Kingdom*, the European Court of Human Rights found this similar—indeed, more sweeping—detention authority, applicable to those who were not always suspected of a crime but were sought to be interrogated for intelligence purposes, to be compatible with the European Convention on Human Rights. The individual right against deprivation of liberty, held the unanimous court, was subordinate to the emergency presented by the terrorist activity found at that point in Northern Ireland.

Is the less expansive detention authority given to the U.S. attorney general under the Patriot Act unconstitutional? Not even the opponents claim this; instead, they merely opine that it raises "constitutional concerns." They say, for example, that the Constitution would be transgressed if the detention power were used to detain those giving "peace training to the IRA." Any statute can be made to raise constitutional concerns if it is manipulated to apply against something other than its constitutional object. Congress is not tasked with drafting against the absurd. It is tasked with addressing the very real dangers of those who wish to kill us for no reason other than that we are American. The attorney general can be given authority to address such hatred. He can also be given the authority to address the risks posed by enemy aliens who may flee or who may seek to thwart our security by exchanging information or launching an additional attack.

But, claim the objectors, the attorney general cannot be given authority to detain persons he cannot deport. Perhaps, but that is not the question that needs to be answered. The attorney general did not ask for that authority. He sought and was given the power to detain those who have been found to be removable. An alien is removable principally when the alien has entered the nation illegally, is in present violation of a previously granted immigration status, or has been engaged in other criminal activity. But for various reasons—mostly related to international obligations that prevent deportation and repatriation to a country where torture is inevitable—being removable is not always the same as being capable of being removed immediately.

So, then, for how long can a removable alien be detained? Under the law prior to the Patriot Act, removable aliens could be detained when "determined by the Attorney General to be a risk to the community or unlikely to comply with the order of removal." This pre–Patriot Act postremoval detention authority was construed by the Supreme Court in *Zadvydas v. Davis*, and the Court suggested six months as a reasonable postremoval detention period.

Yet *Zadvydas*, as a case of statutory interpretation, did not rule out more indefinite detention where risk to community or flight risk is accompanied by special circumstance. The Court explicitly noted that in establishing a presumptive six-month period for detention, it was not denying the government detention beyond this point under unique circumstances. Wrote Justice Breyer for the Court, "Neither do we consider terrorism or other special circumstances where special arguments might be made for forms of preventive detention and for heightened deference to the judgments of the political branches with respect to matters of national security."[4]

The detention by attorney general certification under the Patriot Act should thus not be seen as anomalous or beyond constitutional limit. The attorney general is required to review his certification every six months. Moreover, even the opponents of this highly debated aspect of the act concede that it explicitly provides for judicial review of the attorney general's determination—"Judicial review of any action or decision relating to [detention] (including judicial review of the merits of a determination [by the attorney general that an alien presents a danger to national security]) is available by habeas corpus."[5]

In addition to detention following a removal decision, the Patriot Act provides for short-term detention of a suspected terrorist for up to seven days *before* charging an alien with a crime or a basis for removal. If no charges are filed, the alien is released. Prior to the act, the Immigration and Naturalization Service could detain an alien for forty-eight hours before charging a crime or removable offense. Extending this time of detention without charge does present some legal questions that cannot be fully answered apart from the facts of individual cases. In this respect, whether a constitutional problem is presented by the act likely depends on the extent of due process protection the courts decide must be afforded an individual alien in light of the degree of his or her substantial connection with this country.

## CONCLUSION

Raising civil libertarian objections to new law enforcement provisions is a healthy sign of a vibrant democracy committed to human rights. America should be justly proud of its temperate actions in response to September 11, including its ongoing debate over the proper protection of civil liberties. But no significant constitutional objections have been raised to the USA Patriot Act, either before or after its passage by Congress. Moreover, Congress should be commended for providing a sunset of some of the law enforcement and intelligence authorities that this legislation granted. As Congress has recognized, the possibility of abuse should not obscure the present need and the supposition of trust that one must have if our democratic order is to be safeguarded from those outside our borders who wish to subvert it.

## NOTES

An earlier version of this chapter appeared in *The Responsive Community* 12, no. 1 (winter 2001–2): 56–63.

1. Uniting and Strengthening America by Providing Appropriate Tools Required to Intercept and Obstruct Terrorism Act (USA Patriot Act), H.R. 3162, 107th Cong., 1st sess., October 24, 2001, Sec. 411.

2. *U.S. v. Verdugo-Urquidez*, 494 U.S. 259 (1990).

3. USA Patriot Act, Sec. 412.

4. *Zadvydas v. Davis*, 533 U.S. 678 (2001).

5. USA Patriot Act, Sec. 412.

# Racial Profiling

**9**

# DISCRIMINATION WE'RE AFRAID TO BE AGAINST

## Michael Kinsley

**W**hen thugs menace someone because he looks Arabic, that's racism. When airport security officials single out Arabic-looking men for a more intrusive inspection, that's something else. What is the difference? The difference is that the airport security folks have a rational reason for what they do. An Arab-looking man heading toward a plane is statistically more likely to be a terrorist. That likelihood is infinitesimal, but the whole airport rigmarole is based on infinitesimal chances. If trying to catch terrorists this way makes sense at all, then Willie Sutton logic says you should pay more attention to people who look like Arabs than to people who don't. This is true even if you are free of all ethnic prejudices. It's not racism.

But that doesn't make it okay. Much of the discrimination that is outlawed in this country—correctly outlawed, we (almost) all agree—could be justified, often sincerely, by reasons other than racial prejudice. Without the civil rights laws, employers with nothing personal against blacks might well decide that hiring whites is more cost efficient than judging each job seeker on his or her individual merits. Universities could base their admissions policies on the valid assumption that whites, on average, are better prepared for college. Even though this white advantage is the result of past and present racism, these decisions themselves might be rational and not racially motivated.

All decisions about whom to hire, whom to admit, or whose suitcase to ransack as he's rushing to catch a plane are based on generalizations from observable characteristics to unobservable ones. But even statistically valid generalizations are wrong in particular instances. (Many blacks are better prepared for college than many whites. Virtually every Arab hassled at an airport is not a terrorist.) Because even rational discrimination has victims, and because certain generalizations are especially poisonous, America has decided that these generalizations (about race, gender, religion, and so on) are morally wrong. They are wrong even if they are statistically valid and even if not acting on them imposes a real cost.

Until recently, the term "racial profiling" referred to the police practice of pulling over black male drivers disproportionately on the statistically valid but morally offensive assumption that black male drivers are more likely to be involved in crime. Now the term has become virtually a synonym for racial discrimination. But if "racial profiling" means anything specific at all, it means rational discrimination: racial discrimination with a nonracist rationale. The question is, When is that okay?

The tempting answer is never: Racial discrimination is wrong no matter what the rationale. Period. But today we're at war with a terror network that has killed over 3,000 innocents and has anonymous agents in our country planning more slaughter. Are we really supposed to ignore the one identifiable fact we know about them? That may be asking too much.

And there is another complication in the purist view: affirmative action. You can believe (as I do) that affirmative action is often a justifiable form of discrimination, but you cannot sensibly believe that it isn't discrimination at all. Racial profiling and affirmative action are analytically the same thing. When the cops stop black drivers or companies make extra efforts to hire black employees, they are both giving certain individuals special treatment based on racial generalizations. The only difference is that in one case the special treatment is something bad and in the other it's something good. Yet defenders of affirmative action tend to deplore racial profiling and vice versa.

The truth is that racial profiling and affirmative action are both dangerous medicines that are sometimes appropriate. So when is "sometimes"? It seems obvious to me, though not to many others, that discrimination in favor of historically oppressed groups is less offensive than discrimination against them. Other than that, the considerations are practical. How much is at stake in forbidding a particular act of discrimination? How much is at stake in allowing it?

A generalization from stereotypes may be statistically rational, but is it necessary? When you're storming a plane looking for the person who has planted a bomb somewhere, there isn't time to avoid valid generalizations and treat each person as an individual. At less urgent moments, like airport check-in, the need to use ethnic identity as a shortcut is less obvious. And then there were those passengers in Minneapolis who insisted that three Arab men (who had cleared security) be removed from the plane. These people were making a cost, benefit, and probability analysis so skewed that it amounts to simple racism. (And Northwest Airlines' acquiescence was shameful.)

So what about singling out Arabs at airport security checkpoints? I am skeptical of the value of these check-in rituals in general, which leads me to suspect that the imposition on a minority is not worth it. But assuming these procedures do work, it's hard to argue that helping avoid another September 11 is not worth the imposition, which is pretty small: inconvenience and embarrassment as opposed to losing a job or getting lynched.

A colleague says that people singled out at airport security should be consoled with frequent-flier miles. They're already getting an even better consolation: the huge increase in public sensitivity to anti-Muslim and anti-Arab prejudice, which President Bush—to his enormous credit—has made such a focal point of his response to September 11. And many victims of racial profiling at the airport may not need any consolation. After all, they don't want to be hijacked and blown up, either.

## NOTE

This chapter was originally published in *Slate* magazine, © *Slate*/Distributed by United Feature Syndicate, Inc.

## 10

# A (POTENTIALLY) USEFUL TOOL

## John Derbyshire

**O**ne thing that has become clear since September 11 is that Americans at large are much more tolerant of racial profiling than they were before the terrorists struck. This fact was illustrated shortly after the attacks, on September 20, when three men "of Middle Eastern appearance" were removed from a Northwest Airlines flight because other passengers refused to fly with them. A Northwest spokesman explained that under Federal Aviation Administration rules, "the airline has no choice but to reaccommodate a passenger or passengers if their actions or presence make a majority of passengers uncomfortable and threaten to disrupt normal operations of flight."

Compare this incident with the experience of movie actor James Woods. Woods took a flight from Boston to Los Angeles one week before the World Trade Center attacks. The only other people in first class with him were four men "of Middle Eastern appearance" who acted very strangely. During the entire cross-country flight, none of them had anything to eat or drink, nor did they read or sleep. They only sat upright in their seats, occasionally conversing with each other in low tones. Woods mentioned what he had noticed to a flight attendant who "shrugged it off." Arriving in Los Angeles, Woods told airport authorities, but they "seemed unwilling to become involved." You can see the great change in our attitudes by imagining the consequences if the first incident had happened two weeks earlier or the second two weeks later. The first would then have generated a nationwide storm of indignation about racial profiling and stupendous lawsuits, the second a huge police manhunt for the four men concerned. It seems possible that Woods witnessed a dry run for the attack on the World Trade Center. One of the planes used in that attack was flying the same Boston-to-Los Angeles route that Woods flew. If the authorities had acted on his report—if, that is to say, they had been willing to entertain a little straightforward racial profiling—3,000 lives might have been saved.

Civil libertarians have been warning us that in the current climate of crisis and national peril, our ancient liberties might be sacrificed to the general desire for greater security. They have a point. If truth is the first casualty in war, liberty is often the second. The reason that practically nobody can afford to live in Manhattan who isn't already living there is rent control, a World War II measure, never repealed, that removed a landlord's freedom to let his property at whatever rent the market would bear. But the moral to be drawn from that instance is only that, as legal scholar Bruce Ackerman has argued, emergency legislation must never be enacted without a clear "sunset provision": After some fixed period—Ackerman suggests two years—the law must lapse. The civil liberties crowd does not, in any case, have a dazzling record on the liberties involved in private commercial transactions. What happened to a cabdriver's liberty to use his own judgment about which passengers to pick up? Gone, swept away in the racial profiling panic of the 1990s, along with the lives of several cabbies.

It is in the matter of proactive law enforcement—the kinds of things that police agencies do to prevent crime or terrorism—that our liberties are most at risk in tense times. Whom should you wiretap? Whom should airport security take in for questioning? This is where racial profiling kicks in, with all its ambiguities. Just take a careful look, for example, at that phrase, "of Middle Eastern appearance," which I imagine security agencies are abbreviating "OMEA." In the past when I wrote about this subject, I concentrated on the topics that were in the air at that time: the disproportionate attention police officers give to black and Hispanic persons as crime suspects and the targeting of Wen Ho Lee in the nuclear espionage case. I had nothing to say about terrorists from the Middle East or people who might be thought to look like them. OMEA was not, at that point, an issue.

Now it is, and the problem is that OMEA is perhaps a more dubious description even than "black" or "Hispanic." You can see the difficulties by scanning the photographs of the September 11 hijackers that were published in our newspapers. A few are unmistakably OMEA. My reaction on seeing the photograph of the first to be identified, Mohamed Atta, was that he looked exactly like my own mental conception of an Arab terrorist. On the other hand, one of his companions on American Airlines Flight 11, Wail al-Shehri, is the spitting image of a boy I went to school with—a boy of entirely English origins whose name was Hobson. Ahmed al-Nami (United Airlines Flight 93) looks like a Welsh punk rocker. And so on.

Other visual markers offer similar opportunities for confusion. This fellow with a beard and a turban, coming down the road—he must surely be an Arab or at least a Muslim? Well, maybe, but he is much more likely to be a Sikh—belonging, that is, to a religion that owes more to Hinduism than to Islam, practiced by non-Arab peoples who speak Indo-European languages, and with scriptures written with a Hindi-style script, not an Arabic one. Sikhism requires male adherents to keep an untrimmed beard and wear a turban; Islam does not.

Most other attempts at a "Middle Eastern" typology fail a lot of the time, too. Middle Easterners in the United States are mainly Arabs, right? That depends on where you live. In the state of California, better than half are Iranian or Afghan; in Maryland, practically all are Iranian. Even if you restrict your attention to Americans of Arab origin, stereotypes quickly collapse. You would think it could at least be said with safety that they are mainly Muslims. Not so: More than three-quarters of Arab Americans are Christians. The principal Middle Eastern presence in my own town is St. Mark's Coptic Church. The Copts, who are Egyptian Christians, are certainly OMEA, and they speak Arabic for nonliturgical purposes and have Arabic names. They have little reason to identify with Muslim terrorists, however, having been rudely persecuted by extremist Muslims in their homeland for decades. Misconceptions cut the other way, too. Care to guess what proportion of Muslim Americans are of Arab origins? Answer: around one in eight. Most American Muslims are black.

That we could impose any even halfway reasonable system of "racial profiling" on this chaos seems impossible. Yet we can where it matters most, and I believe we should—certainly in airport security, which, as a matter of fact, is where OMEA profiling began during the hijack scares of the early 1970s. When boarding a plane, documents need to be presented, names declared, words exchanged. This gives security officials a much richer supply of data than a mere "eyeball" check. We return here to the point, as affirmed by the U.S. Supreme Court, that "race"—which is to say, visible physical characteristics typical of, or at least frequent among, some group with a common origin—can be used as part of a suspect profile to identify targets for further investigation, provided there are other criteria in play.

We should profile at airports because, as the James Woods incident shows, profiling is an aid—very far from an infallible one but still a useful one—to identifying those who want to harm us in this as in any other area of law enforcement. To pretend that any person passing through airport security is as likely as any other to be a hijacker is absurd, just as it is absurd to pretend that any driver on the New Jersey Turnpike is as likely as any other to be transporting narcotics.

Crises like the present one can generate hysteria, it is true, but they can also have a clarifying effect on our outlook, sweeping away the wishful thinking of easier times, exposing the hollowness of relativism and moral equivalence, and forcing us to the main point. And peacetime has its own hysterias. I believe that when the long peace that ended on September 11 comes into perspective, we shall see that the fuss about racial profiling was, ultimately, hysterical, driven by a dogmatic and unreasoned refusal to face up to group differences. So long as the authorities treat everyone with courtesy and apologize to the inconvenienced innocent, racial profiling is a practical and perfectly sensible tool for preventing crime and terrorism.

## NOTE

This chapter was originally published in the *National Review*, © 2001 by National Review, Inc., 215 Lexington Avenue, New York, NY 10016. Reprinted by permission.

# Freedom of the Press versus National Security

# MILITARY SECRETS AND THE FIRST AMENDMENT

## C. Robert Zelnick

**O**n June 26, 1993, the U.S. Navy launched twenty-three Tomahawk cruise missiles at Iraq's military intelligence headquarters in Al Mansour, an affluent suburb of Baghdad, to retaliate for Saddam Hussein's alleged plot to kill former President George Bush during the latter's visit to Kuwait. That afternoon, the late Secretary of Defense Les Aspin joined President Bill Clinton, National Security Adviser Anthony Lake, and others in the Oval Office. They hoped to get early confirmation that the missiles had struck the intended target. As might have been expected, television sets were tuned to CNN, but this time with an even greater sense of urgency because U.S. reconnaissance satellites were not favorably positioned to monitor the results of the attack.

When the intended time for the strike passed with no news reports of unusual activity, Secretary Aspin called General Colin Powell at the Pentagon command center. "Could the Tomahawks possibly have missed?" asked the worried secretary.

"Not all of them," replied Powell.

In "desperation," presidential assistant David Gergen called Tom Johnson, president of CNN News. Gergen informed Johnson about the launch and asked him to check with his man in Baghdad in case the reporter had slept through the attack.

The inquiry did not come at the most fortuitous moment for Johnson. His reporters had apprised him only a day or two earlier that a military reprisal against Iraq was likely. However, CNN had not been able to get its own satellite uplink closer than Amman, Jordan, and was relying solely on its radio stringer in the Iraqi capital. In addition, Johnson had a policy against providing the government with information not reported on the air. Like countless other Western journalists and news executives operating in nations with no tradition of political freedom, he knew officials in such nations tend to "mirror image" the relationship between the press and the government. They assume the former to be an adjunct of the latter as active intelligence services when operating abroad. While working in such countries, Johnson took extra care not to reinforce such perceptions.

Johnson had just received reports that missiles were striking the outskirts of Baghdad, some hitting the intelligence facility and others missing. With the information about to go on the air, Johnson bent his policy to the extent of apprising the White House what CNN was "reporting." Moments later, a relieved White House watched as CNN confirmed the story.

The incident, related to me by Secretary Aspin some months later and confirmed by Johnson, reflects one small part of one small piece of a complex mosaic. The relationship between the national security apparatus, including the military, and the press is at times symbiotic, at times antagonistic. It is sometimes described as an "adversarial relationship," but the description would be accurate only if the media and the military were aligned on opposite sides. This, of course, has never been the case. Rather, each has its own role to play, and while each is ultimately a guardian of national freedom and democratic values, their separate missions sometimes put them at cross-purposes.

But we are not talking about a zero-sum game. The press seeks to acquire and disseminate as much relevant information as possible. The military regards information as one among many variables to use and control. Too often the issue is described simplistically as a conflict between First Amendment rights and national security. Both history and experience teach the error of this formulation. While it is certainly possible for a careless dispatch to jeopardize legitimate national security interests, military operations, and the lives of service personnel, the documented instances of such reporting are exceedingly few. In dozens of wars and military operations over the past hundred years, representatives of the press have been privy to highly classified operational details or learned or observed things that could compromise legitimate security needs. In nearly all instances, they acted with restraint and responsibility.

## POINTS OF CONFLICT

Documented incidents of reporting that actually harmed the U.S. military or security interests are nonexistent, although there are a handful of instances where irresponsible press conduct could have produced serious harm. During World War II in the Pacific, for example, the *Chicago Tribune* published a report from one of its Pacific correspondents, Stanley Johnson, listing the names of the Japanese warships involved in the Battle of Midway. This information could only have come from coded Japanese communications intercepted and "cracked" by U.S. intelligence. Fortunately, the Japanese failed to read the *Chicago Tribune* and did not alter their encryption regime.

In Korea, General MacArthur's brilliant landing at Inchon was reported before the troops actually hit shore, but again, no damage.

During the Vietnam War, the press had virtually unfettered access to any part of the country, and there was no censorship. Still the media behaved responsibly. When interviewed by the late Peter Braestrup for his definitive study of media–military relations, *Battle Lines,* Barry Zorthian, former spokesman for the U.S. military in Vietnam, stated, "Our leverage was the lifting of credentials, and that was done in only four or five cases, and at least two or three of these were unintentional errors on the part of the correspondent."[1]

Past efforts to control press coverage of military operations and related matters is a history of inconsistency often rooted more in the whims of individual commanders than logic. Prior to the Civil War, the press faced few, if any, restrictions on its coverage of military operations. The relatively few journalists covering combat and the primitive transportation and communications technologies were decisive checks on the potential to compromise operational details. The development of the telegraph during the 1850s changed that. During the Civil War,

Union Generals Ambrose Burnside and William T. Sherman either denied access completely to journalists or kept them at a considerable distance from the story. Meanwhile, an ad hoc censorship regime proved powerful enough to shut down the *Chicago Times* for its incessant attacks on President Lincoln.

When the United States entered World War I in April 1917, the State, Navy, and War Departments established the Committee on Public Information to provide information and enforce censorship regulations. Voluntarily accepted by the press, the regulations forbade publication of such information as "troop movements within the United States, ship sailings, and the identification of units dispatched overseas."[2] In addition, Congress passed the Espionage Act of 1917, which prohibited publication of information useful to the enemy or any interference with military operations or war production, and the Sedition Act of 1918, which banned critical remarks about the conduct of operations, the U.S. government, or its military forces, including the flag. In each case, penalties could include imprisonment for up to twenty years and fines up to $10,000. Press dispatches from the war zone were initially subjected to censorship by a single former *New York Herald* reporter and Associated Press correspondent, Frederick Palmer, and later by a committee of former journalists commissioned as reserve Army officers. The process functioned chaotically. The committee ultimately revoked the credentials of five of the sixty journalists assigned to cover the war. None of this prevented a United Press International reporter from prematurely breaking a story that the armistice had been signed, a breach of security that resulted in the committee temporarily blocking communication between the reporter and his New York headquarters.

Immediately after Pearl Harbor, Congress enacted the War Powers Act, which included the creation of an Office of Censorship. The new office quickly promulgated guidelines, later codified into the Code of Wartime Practices, which took effect January 15, 1942. This code implemented essentially the same types of security restrictions applied during World War I but without the Espionage and Sedition Acts. Throughout the war, the code governed journalists in most combat zones, including the European and North African theaters. In the Pacific, General Douglas MacArthur and the Navy's chief of operations, Admiral Ernest J. King, imposed additional restraints on the press. In fact, years later, the Gannett Foundation's "Media at War" report explained that

> MacArthur required each correspondent's copy to go through a multiple censorship review before being released, and pressured journalists to produce stories that burnished the image of the troops and their supreme commander. The Navy, for its part, delayed the release of news, frequently waiting until a story of combat success could be paired with one describing a setback.[3]

## TURNING POINTS: VIETNAM

Vietnam marked a turning point in relations between the military and the press. It was the first military conflict subject to daily television coverage. Only a few hardy reporters initially covered the conflict, but by 1968, more than 2,000 accredited reporters were involved. During the conflict, the press routinely applied the term "credibility gap" to military claims of progress. Many in the military blamed the press for loss of public support for the conflict and the resultant political restrictions on its conduct.

Throughout Vietnam, accredited journalists came and went as they pleased. They "hitchhiked" on military transports and helicopters when available and made their own arrangements where necessary. There was virtually no censorship. Instead, the Military Assistance Command, Vietnam (MACV), headquarters for the U.S. effort, asked journalists to refrain from reporting items such as planned offensives, troop movements, and the participation of allied forces in particular operations.

In a technical sense, the rules worked well. Of the thousands of correspondents covering the war, only a handful committed military guideline violations severe enough to result in the revocation of credentials, and only two violations seriously jeopardized operations or safety.

The problem in Vietnam was the deteriorating political relationship between the press and the military. This was partly a reflection and partly a cause of the mounting opposition to the war in the United States. For members of the press, the daily briefings at the Joint U.S. Public Affairs Office (JUSPAO), the office established by MACV to dispense information on the overall effort and supervise coverage by in-country members of the American and foreign media, became known as the "Five O'Clock Follies." This was because briefers often exaggerated political progress and manufactured military victories and enemy casualties. Facetiously, Western newsmen often said, "If it's Vietnamese and it's dead, JUSPAO calls it a Vietcong." As the war continued, reports on the "tactical evacuation" of Vietnamese civilians from their villages; the widespread use of napalm, "Agent Orange," and other defoliants or herbicides; the occasional allied atrocity; the ability of the enemy to mount major operations such as the 1968 Tet offensive; and the horrendous U.S. casualties undoubtedly had a profound impact on public opinion in the United States.

## GRENADA

The Grenada operation began with a lie and deteriorated from there. In October 1983, Ronald Reagan was president. Platoon leaders and company commanders of Vietnam were now the bird colonels. The media's standing had fallen precipitately. For example, a survey found that in 1966, 29 percent of respondents had "a great deal of confidence" in people running the media. That figure fell to 19 percent in 1983, the year of the Grenada invasion (and to 11 percent in 1995).[4] The military took advantage of the fortuitous political circumstances, virtually barring press coverage of the operation, which, contrary to the Pentagon's first accounts, was characterized by spotty intelligence, logistical foulups, and bungled execution. In fact, as Peter Braestrup recalls, CBS White House correspondent Bill Plante learned of the operation from a source the day before the invasion. He sought confirmation from White House Press Secretary Larry Speakes, who vetted the information with Bob Sims, the National Security Council press officer, and Admiral John Poindexter, the president's national security adviser. From Poindexter, the word came: "Plante—no invasion of Grenada. Preposterous. Knock it down hard."[5]

Compare that lie with the attitude of Brigadier General Robert A. Mc-Clure, the assistant chief of staff at the Supreme Headquarters Allied European Force. Asked whether the Allies should mislead the press regarding the date and location of the Normandy invasion, Braestrup quotes from McClure's note to Sir Cyril Radcliffe of the British Ministry of Information: "Men who profess to present the news honestly should not be subjected to official suasion to present it dishonestly, however laudable the purpose. We cannot remove the foundations of a house and expect it to remain standing."[6] The Allies found other ways to disinform the Germans.

It is possible to see World War II coverage in too rosy a light. After all, the press was usually uniformed, censorship was strict, and reporters were subject to military courts-martial for disobedience. But the access was near total, from amphibious landings to paratroop drops behind enemy lines. Denials of access, beginning with Grenada, had no reasonable military basis. As Major General Winant Sidle, U.S. Army (ret.), who headed a committee that developed procedures governing press activities for military conflicts after Grenada, candidly acknowledged, "Although never admitted, the military's distrust of the media at the time of the Grenada operation in 1983 had to be part of the reason the media were not permitted on Grenada for the first two days, and only a pool was allowed on the third day."[7]

In response, Joint Chiefs of Staff Chairman General John W. Vessey appointed the Sidle Commission, formally known as the Chairman of the Joint Chiefs of Staff Media Military Relations Panel. The commission reviewed the Grenada experience and recommended a more appropriate way for dealing with future operations. Comments from the press were solicited. In his letter to General Sidle dated January 3, 1984, Roone Arledge, president of ABC News, noted,

> On the day our troops landed on Grenada, I wrote to Secretary of Defense Weinberger, saying the practice of journalists accompanying American troops into action was as old as our republic. Now, for the first time in our history, the press was unreasonably excluded from going with American troops into action. In my opinion, no convincing or compelling reason has yet been cited for this unprecedented departure from our tradition of independent press reporting.[8]

On August 23, 1984, General Sidle's panel unanimously concluded that "it is essential that the U.S. news media cover U.S. military operations to the maximum degree possible consistent with mission security and the safety of U.S. forces."[9] The panel emphasized that the preferred method of coverage is open access for all journalists assigned to cover the story.

The panel also recognized that the pool is necessary to handle atypical situations, as when operations are in remote or otherwise inaccessible areas.

The panel concluded that an adversarial relationship between the press and the military "is healthy" but that "mutual antagonism and distrust are not in the best interests of the media, the military, or the American people."[10] Michael Burch, assistant secretary of defense for public affairs, responded to the Sidle recommendations by saying, "We agree with them all."[11] Secretary of Defense Caspar Weinberger and General Vessey formed a "public affairs cell" in the office of the chairman of the Joint Chiefs of Staff to put the recommendations into practice.

## PANAMA

The only test of the Pentagon's good faith in implementing the Sidle recommendations came during the Panama invasion of December 1989. By any reasonable standard, the military clearly flunked. The Pentagon operated the pool out of Washington and notified the media only a few hours before the commencement of the operation. About four hours before the Pentagon pool landed in Panama, U.S. forces started their attacks against priority targets.

Once the pool landed, its members were effectively kept from the action for at least thirty-six hours, longer than in Grenada. The delay left little of the story remaining except the search for the hiding Noriega. The military could have used helicopters to transport the press, but helicopters were appropriated for higher-priority operations. This clearly indicated that plans to accommodate the pool and other journalists received inadequate attention prior to commencement of the operation. Sniper fire prevented ground transportation. The military failed to provide pool reporters timely briefings on the operation's status. Instead, they were subjected to political backgrounders by U.S. Embassy officials. The military also prevented photographers from shooting pictures of closed caskets bearing the remains of U.S. servicemen killed in action as they were prepared for shipment home.

Interestingly, all the secrecy did not prevent the press from reporting a flurry of activity at U.S. bases prior to the start of the operation. And it did not prevent at least one CNN report that the operation may be under way.

Years earlier, the Supreme Court had admonished in *Near v. Minnesota*, "No one would question but that a government might prevent actual obstruction to its recruiting service or the publication of the sailing dates of transports or the number and location of troops."[12] Here, however, two observations are in order. First, with the exception of communications involved in activating the Pentagon pool, the government did not make any efforts, either in Panama or in other recent operations, to alert publishers, executive producers, or senior press officials about imminent operations and to request editorial restraint. Although informal working-level communications were present, the kind of high-level effort needed to ensure operational secrecy was never undertaken. Second, despite the breach in operational security, which in wars past would have been grounds for profound concern, no recent broadcasts or reports appear to have benefited any U.S. enemy on the battlefield in Panama or elsewhere. Today's troop departures, whether by plane or ship, are so widely publicized that the very notion that "publication of the sailing dates of [troop] transports or the number and location of troops" might provide some advantage to any enemy sounds almost quaint.

The reason is that the United States today does not have enemies capable of interfering with its mastery of the high seas, or, for that matter, the skies. Tactical operations today are accompanied by efforts to suppress enemy air defenses, blind the enemy to advancing troops, impede its communications, and intercept its own troop movements. Coupled with the ability of the United States to strike from beyond the range of enemy interference, the likelihood of press leaks actually causing damage is, in the most likely contingencies, remote.

## THE PERSIAN GULF WAR

Coverage of the Persian Gulf War involved efforts by at least 1,400 reporters trying to gain access to military personnel in the field. Some journalists were stationed in Baghdad, while others—the regular core of Pentagon, State Department, White House, and Washington journalists—remained in Washington and hoped to gain information or insight from there. Before the start of Operation Desert Storm, Louis A. "Pete" Williams, the Department of Defense's assistant secretary for public affairs, issued guidelines for coverage with restrictions that fell into familiar and acceptable categories. The press could not provide coverage regarding specific numbers of troops, aircraft, or weapons systems; details of future plans, operations, or strikes; information on the specific location of military forces or security arrangements in effect; rules of engagement; intelligence collection activities; troop movements; identification of aircraft origin; effectiveness or ineffectiveness of enemy camouflage, cover, deception, or targeting; specific information on downed aircraft or damaged ships while search-and-rescue missions were planned or under way; and information on operational or support vulnerabilities of U.S. and allied forces.

By all accounts, including the Pentagon's, the U.S. military handled the press poorly. Then–Secretary of Defense Dick Cheney set the tone initially when he refused to let reporters accompany the first U.S. troops to the region on August 8, 1990, because Saudi Arabia declined to permit it. Several months after the war, a committee of seventeen senior news executives from the networks, leading wire services, newspapers, and weeklies circulated a fourteen-page report on the military's handling of the press titled "Independent Reporting: Prevention Of."[13]

Still, the media tried to get as much of the story as possible. Those who could assigned reporters to Baghdad. Many print reporters braved military resistance and operated unilaterally, as did such network correspondents as Forest Sawyer of ABC News, who eventually linked up with advancing Egyptian units, and Bob McKeown of CBS, who became the first television correspondent to report live from liberated Kuwait City. Both Sawyer's and McKeown's work provided a hint of the next stage in the difficult media–military relationship as the media's ability to report in real time came increasingly in conflict with the legitimate military need to avoid presenting the other side with instant battlefield intelligence. Throughout the Persian Gulf War, however, most reporters on the scene were reduced to sitting through press briefings in Riyadh asking questions that reflected the silliness and hostility of the situation.

## AFGHANISTAN

It is interesting to compare the highly restricted coverage of Operation Desert Shield and Operation Desert Storm with the work of the press in reporting on the Shiite and Kurdish rebellions after the war. With no pools, no escorts, no "restricted" areas, and no "Saudi sensibilities" to worry about, journalists, in the full exercise of their First Amendment rights, documented the horrors being perpetrated by Saddam Hussein and countenanced by the Bush administration. The result was a prompt and substantial change in U.S. policy, which the president and his advisers would later attribute not to the media but to the desire to keep Iraq's Kurds from flooding neighboring Turkey. For more than a year following the cessation of hostilities in the Persian Gulf, Pentagon officials and a committee consisting mainly of the same individuals who had published the "Independent Reporting" document reviewed the experience. They sought to reach an accord on new and more satisfactory procedures to govern future conflicts. Eventually, they agreed on nine principles—including the stipulations that "journalists will have access to all major military units" and that "military public affairs officers should act as liaisons but should not interfere with the reporting process"—and "agreed to disagree" over the question of "prior security review," or censorship.

Then came Afghanistan, and, at least in its early days, most of the good intentions were relegated to their traditional mission, paving the road to hell. Reporters had difficulty gaining access to the carriers supporting the operation or the pilots returning from strike missions. Bases in nearby Uzbekistan and Tajikistan were off limits because of local sensibilities. Accompanying special forces was out of the question. Reporters at one base camp were herded into a warehouse to keep them away from troops returning from a "friendly fire" accident. On one occasion, a *Washington Post* reporter was stopped at gunpoint from inspecting collateral damage from bombs dropped by an unmanned U.S. drone. As the war continued and U.S. success mounted, access became somewhat easier.

## A MINIMAL THREAT

While conflicts between First Amendment values and national security needs are a long-running source of legal analysis and intellectual fascination, during the past generation it has become clear that such conflicts are truly aberrational. The press rarely poses any kind of danger to national security. The goal of defense officials, military or civilian, who seek to keep the press on a short leash is, in most instances, to control the editorial slant of what is reported rather than to protect tactical, strategic, or national security from the unauthorized disclosure of sensitive material.

As exhibited in operations as varied as Grenada, Panama, the Persian Gulf, and Afghanistan, the method most often chosen by the military to control the press is to limit timely access to bases or combat operations. This practice is, as reemphasized by post–Persian Gulf War lawsuits, difficult to oppose through the mechanism of First Amendment litigation. By the time they reach the courts, such First Amendment complaints may be held moot. Courts, moreover, are hesitant to substitute their judgment on matters of asserted security for that of base or field commanders. While media access to military bases and operations may be a First Amendment value, it has yet to be held a First Amendment right. Further, since both the Pentagon's military and civilian leadership and the most powerful representatives of the media tend to form part of the Washington establishment, it is my sense that they dislike potentially damaging political or legal confrontations. Thus, they generally choose to resolve their differences through such amicable mechanisms as panels and joint committees pointed toward the next conflict rather than seeking to redress grievances over the last one. Such was certainly the case following Grenada, the Persian Gulf War, and arguably after Panama.

One must recognize that most of the problems within the past dozen years trace back to the period of mutual contempt and suspicion that grew out of the Vietnam era. That legacy seems to be finally fading. While no specific post-Vietnam plan for coverage of combat operations has worked well to date, the hard work and spirit of mutual respect that characterized the adoption of the "nine principles" offers some hope for the future.

## NOTES

An earlier version of this chapter appeared in the inaugural issue of the *University of Mississippi Journal of National Security Law* in December 1997.

1. Peter Braestrup, *Battle Lines* (New York: Priority Press Publications, 1985), 65.

2. Everette E. Dennis et al., Gannett Foundation Report, "The Media at War: The Press and the Persian Gulf Conflict," June 1991, 9.

3. Ibid., 11.

4. Humphrey Taylor, "Some Positive News for a Change: Confidence in Leaders of Institutions Improves Somewhat," *Harris Poll* 1996, no. 10: 1–3. Each year Louis Harris & Associates Inc. conducts the *Harris Poll,* a survey that tracks the public confidence in the leaders of twelve major American institutions.

5. Braestrup, 89.

6. Personal correspondence from Brigadier General Robert A. McClure to Sir Cyril Radcliffe, February 9, 1944. In Braestrup, 31.

7. Major General Winant Sidle, U.S. Army (ret.), "A Battle behind the Scenes: Gulf War Reheats Military-Media Controversy," *Military Review* (September 1991): 55.

8. Letter from Roone Arledge, president of ABC News, submitted to General Winant Sidle, Chairman of the Joint Chiefs of Staff Media-Military Relations Panel, January 3, 1984.

9. Gerald F. Seib, "Pentagon Says It Will Study Plan to Let Reporters Accompany Troops into Battle," *Wall Street Journal,* August 24, 1984, A1.

10. Richard Halloran, "Pentagon Issues New Guidelines for Combat Zones," *New York Times,* August 24, 1984, A1.

11. Ibid.

12. *Near v. Minnesota,* 283 U.S. 697 (1931).

13. "Covering the Persian Gulf War: Independent Reporting: Prevention Of," July 1, 1991. Unpublished report, on file with the *Journal of National Security Law.*

**(12)**

# PATRIOTS AND PROFESSIONALS: JOURNALISTS AS RESPONSIBLE CITIZENS

## Steven V. Roberts

**S**hould the press be objective or patriotic? Does it have to choose between the demands of professionalism and citizenship? Those questions have always been asked in journalism classes and think tank seminars, but they have taken on a new urgency since the attacks of September 11. For the foreseeable future, the media will be reporting on military strikes, strategy, and secrets. Every day, journalists will have to balance two real and competing virtues: the public's right to know and the military's right to protect lives and security.

As a working journalist for almost forty years and as a professor who teaches journalistic ethics, I have two basic answers to these questions. First of all, there is no inherent conflict between patriotism and professionalism, so there is no need to choose between them. The highest form of patriotism is for journalists to do their job, a job that is defined and defended by the First Amendment. Simply agreeing with the government—any government—is not the only way to express patriotism. Posing questions, raising concerns, exposing mistakes, and voicing dissent are much harder tasks and more essential to the national interest.

My second answer is this: Along with the rights that journalists enjoy under the Constitution come enormous responsibilities. The two are inseparable. As the Supreme Court ruled in the Pentagon papers case, the

government has virtually no ability to stop the press from printing anything in this country. But the press must use its freedom wisely and well.
The cases where the military can justifiably withhold information from
the press are rare; the cases where the press can justifiably withhold information from readers and viewers are even more rare. But they are
real. Without journalistic self-restraint, democracy cannot work and the
public interest cannot be served.

## FINDING THE BALANCE

Most news consumers have no idea that the press takes such questions
seriously. I constantly hear the refrain, *You only want to sell papers, or
boost ratings.* But the public only knows what is finally printed or broadcast; they seldom know what is not released, so they don't understand
that the media engage in balancing acts all the time. And the most difficult and important balancing acts involve coverage of national security.
Citizens deserve information about the state of their country's readiness,
its success on the battlefield, and its future planning. It is their tax dol-
lars that finance any conflict and their children who fight and die in their
nation's service. But secrecy is sometimes necessary to maintain sur-
prise, protect intelligence sources, or confuse an enemy. So how can
America have both openness and security? Can these values coexist?

My answer is emphatically yes, but it's important to remember that
journalism is an imperfect process. There is no code of press conduct
handed down to Moses—or even Edward R. Murrow—and inscribed
on stone tablets. Principles have to be applied and adjusted to changing
circumstances. But one useful version of those principles was articu-
lated by Leonard Downie Jr., the longtime editor of the *Washington
Post,* in an interview with the *New York Times* a month after September
11. A "handful of times," he said, the administration had "raised concerns" to *Post* editors about specific stories they were planning. "In
some instances," he explained, "we have kept out of stories certain facts
that we agreed could be detrimental to national security and not instrumental to our readers, such as methods of intelligence collection."[1]

Downie has set up a two-part test before "certain facts" can be with-
held. They have to be "detrimental" to national security, not just em-

barrassing or inconvenient. And they should not be "instrumental" to the tasks of citizenship, holding leaders and their policies accountable. Ethical decision making in the real world is not a question of theological debate but a process of constantly weighing costs against benefits. How valuable is the information to the public? What damage would its release entail? Which choice produces the greatest public good?

Here is an example of how that process plays out in practice. When I worked at *U.S. News,* one of our reporters in the Persian Gulf learned the details of the imminent counteroffensive against Saddam Hussein's troops that were occupying Kuwait. As the editors weighed the costs and benefits of printing the story, the decision was soon obvious: The information would clearly be "detrimental" to the safety of U.S. forces but not "instrumental" to our readers. As a result, the story never ran. But our readers had no idea the debate had even taken place.

Another example occurred when a U.S. pilot was shot down during the air phase of the Persian Gulf War. Did the public have a right to know about the episode? Yes. It deserved a fair accounting of how the war was going, good and bad. But did the public have a right to know exactly where and when the pilot went down? No. Those facts were not necessary to the story, but they could have seriously compromised any attempt to rescue the flyer.

This process of journalistic deliberation depends heavily on the interaction between the press and the government, and that interaction is clouded by deeply held suspicions on both sides. Both institutions regard Vietnam as their historical touchstone, but they draw exactly opposite lessons from that traumatic period. The military basically believes that reporters can't be trusted because they will reveal information that could help lose the war. Don Oberdorfer, a veteran foreign correspondent, put it this way: "A whole generation of military officers grew up believing that the press was the problem, if not the enemy."[2] And a whole generation of journalists grew up believing the same thing about the military brass—they were the enemy because they would always lie to cover up their own mistakes.

At the same time, the press and the Pentagon need each other and manage to form a working relationship despite these animosities. When Admiral Bobby Ray Inman was selected to be secretary of defense by the first President Bush, a fascinating story leaked out. For many years, Inman functioned as an informal conduit between Washington journalists and the Pentagon. No reporter or editor wanted to ask the military for an official opinion about a story—that would be giving up too much power. But no one wanted to ignore the possibility of damaging some ongoing mission or intelligence operation. So they would call Inman—who never did survive Senate confirmation—and ask for an informal advisory on whether a story would cause the Pentagon problems. That kind of relationship was essential for a fair weighing of costs and benefits, and it worked for both sides. Even today, some form of back-channel communication still exists. That's how Downie is able to get a read on whether "certain facts" in stories about terrorism are "detrimental" or not.

## CONTEMPORARY CASES

The war on terrorism contains a number of case studies that illustrate how this relationship works. The Pentagon argues that it does its best to accommodate reporters but that many missions in Afghanistan and elsewhere require both stealth and secrecy. Immediately before the military campaign in Afghanistan, Rear Admiral Craig Quigley, a Pentagon spokesman, explained to the *New York Times,* "There is an extraordinary sensitivity to telegraphing any sort of time line or destination or capability, because we are going to be fighting such an unconventional foe."[3] That's a fair point. Doyle McManus, Washington bureau chief of the *Los Angeles Times,* spoke for most responsible journalists when he said, "It's pretty easy to see that we're not going to have real-time reporting or verification of commando raids or covert action. I don't think that most of us ever expected to. And in those areas the restrictions on their face are quite reasonable."[4]

In the view of many editors and reporters, however, the Pentagon has been far too restrictive in its policies toward the press, limiting access to battlefields and combat units when such limits are not justified by security considerations. In December 2001, American journalists visiting a forward base in Afghanistan were physically prevented from interviewing, or even seeing, survivors of a friendly-fire episode. No security was involved, just the reputations of the officers who had made the error. As

Walter Rodgers of CNN noted, "It was an egregious incident in news management."[5] The Pentagon later apologized, but the mind-set of the officers on the ground was clear: The press is the enemy.

That same mind-set displayed itself when Doug Struck of the *Washington Post* tried to check out reports of civilian casualties in a remote mountain village. He claims he was turned away at gunpoint by American soldiers; the Pentagon says the soldiers were only trying to guarantee Struck's safety. Struck sticks by his version and insists, "The important thing isn't whether Doug Struck was threatened. It shows the extremes the military is going to to keep this war secret, to keep reporters from finding out what's going on."[6]

Attempts to control information go well beyond the battlefield. In October 2001, the *Washington Post* reported that intelligence briefers had told members of Congress that there was a "high probability" of another major terrorist attack and a "100 percent chance" of such an attack if America struck back at Afghanistan.[7] The administration was furious at the leak and severely restricted future briefings to Congress, an order they later rescinded. But Downie justified his decision this way: "We decided to run the story because it was news of importance to our readers. The substance of the story did not endanger lives nor compromise national security. On the contrary, if it made Americans more alert to possible dangers, it could help save lives."[8]

## NEW PRECAUTIONS

Despite its complaints against the Pentagon, the press cannot forget its obligations to act responsibly and take the military's concerns seriously. This is particularly true at a time when new technology makes it increasingly possible for the media to broadcast live from almost anywhere, including remote battlefields. During Vietnam, it took a minimum of twenty-four hours to get scenes of combat to American television sets. Today, satellite uplinks and video phones have changed the rules and raised the stakes. Journalists have to be more careful than ever to safeguard the security of the troops they are covering.

In the aftermath of September 11, journalists also have to be much more aware of providing information that can be useful to terrorists. A good example: Experts fear that terrorists could hijack a crop-dusting plane, load it with deadly bacteria, and contaminate a wide area. Should we publish stories detailing the possibility of such attacks? Absolutely. Such information is clearly "instrumental" to public safety. People who guard airports or service planes could provide useful intelligence about suspicious characters. But should we publish details about which planes or nozzle technology could do the most damage in the hands of hijackers? Absolutely not. Those facts could clearly be "detrimental" to public safety without providing any real value to the public.

Then there is the case of Osama bin Laden. The administration was concerned that television networks were simply taking any tape he provided and throwing it on the air immediately without any editing or judgment. The result was to give the terrorist leader enormous stature and a powerful platform from which to spread his anti-American venom. Condoleezza Rice, the national security adviser, asked network executives to show more restraint in broadcasting future bin Laden broadsides.

This was a tough call. On one hand, no one has a right to total access to the airwaves, not even the president. Said press critic Tom Rosenstiel in the *Washington Post*, "Journalists are being forced by the government to think. The notion that you have to be first on the air with some junk, before you even review it, is nonsense."[9] On the other hand, journalists have to be extremely wary of government pressure and attempts at censorship. Bin Laden might be a hateful and dangerous figure, but he is an extremely significant one, and learning about him is certainly essential to an informed public.

The media has a right to print or broadcast anything about bin Laden, but what's the responsible balance? In my view, it's this: You provide enough information so that Americans have ample opportunity to understand who he is and what he represents. But you don't simply turn over your airwaves or news columns and let him rant at any length he chooses. Keep him in the proper perspective. That's what professional journalists do every day: apply their training and experience and make judgments about what's important and what's not.

## ETERNAL VIGILANCE

Making these judgments is a never-ending process. Every day, journalists go through the same balancing act, and every day, conditions change. Before September 11, bin Laden rated very little coverage by the American media. During the 2000 presidential campaign, George W. Bush got exactly one question about the Taliban. After September 11, the calculations about bin Laden's importance shifted sharply. Before September 11, no one cared about crop-duster technology; suddenly, that information became vital to national security.

But if conditions constantly change, two verities do not. Journalists must stay vigilant, protecting their rights and their obligations to keep the public informed and their leaders accountable—even at gunpoint in the mountains of Afghanistan. But journalists must also remember that our rights flourish only in a free society and that we have an obligation to keep that society safe and secure. The First Amendment, to quote one sage observation, is not a suicide pact. And the military is not the enemy.

Perhaps the best we can hope for is an uneasy truce where each institution, the media and the military, try to understand each other's requirements and responsibilities. Most journalists are as patriotic as any gung ho Marine. They just show their patriotism in different ways. And both of their jobs are vital to a healthy and secure nation.

## NOTES

1. Bill Carter and Felicity Barringer, "Networks Agree to U.S. Request to Edit Future bin Laden Tapes," *New York Times*, October 11, 2001, A1.

2. Elizabeth Becker, "In the War on Terrorism, a Battle to Shape Opinion," *New York Times*, November 11, 2002, B5.

3. Felicity Barringer and Jim Rutenberg, "The News Media Make Ready for War," *New York Times*, October 1, 2001, C1.

4. Felicity Barringer, "Reporters Want More Access, but Are Careful to Ask Nicely," *New York Times*, October 22, 2001, B3.

5. Frank Rich, "Freedom from the Press," *New York Times*, March 2, 2002, A15.

6. Howard Kurtz, "War Coverage Takes a Negative Turn; Civilian Deaths, Military Errors Become Focus as Reporters Revisit Bombing Sites," *Washington Post*, February 17, 2002, A14.

7. Susan Schmidt and Bob Woodward, "FBI, CIA Warn Congress of More Attacks as Blair Details Case against Bin Laden; Retaliation Feared If U.S. Strikes Afghanistan," *Washington Post*, October 5, 2001, A1.

8. Michael Getler, "Bush and the Bacon-Cooler," *Washington Post*, October 14, 2001, B6.

9. Paul Farhi, "The Networks, Giving Aid to the Enemy?; Unedited Bin Laden Video Sparks Debate," *Washington Post*, October 12, 2001, C1.

# Public Health

# 13

# PUBLIC HEALTH IN THE AGE
# OF BIOTERRORISM: A DIALOGUE

*The following is an edited transcript of a dialogue organized by the
Communitarian Network on public health and bioterrorism. It was held
at the National Press Club on October 26, 2001. The participants were
Alan Kraut, professor of history at American University; Fitzhugh Mullan, a clinical professor of pediatrics and public health at The George
Washington University; and Richard Riegelman, professor of epidemiol-
ogy and biostatistics and the founding dean of The George Washington
University School of Public Health and Health Services. Amitai Etzioni
moderated the discussion.*

**AMITAI ETZIONI:** Ladies and gentlemen, welcome to a communitarian
dialogue on the ethical and legal issues raised by bioterrorism. Because
one of the issues we are most concerned with as communitarians is the
delicate and difficult balance between individual rights and the common
good, we are concerned both with protecting our rights and with protecting the health of our people.

A place where many discussions on this issue start is with the scenario
of a terrorist group infecting a large number of people with smallpox.
Let's stipulate that smallpox is highly infectious, that it has a high fatality
rate (30 percent), and that there is a period in which you have symptoms

but you are not yet contagious. In most of the scenarios, you come to a situation where very quickly a very large number—hundreds of thousands, millions—of people are infected. And then the question is how to stop the plague. Some people call for an education campaign, some for quarantining. It's choosing from the range of voluntary to coercive means that we are so concerned with today.

## PERSONAL RISK VERSUS THE COMMON GOOD

**AE:** Before we even discuss the attack itself, let's talk about preventive vaccination campaigns. When we had various forms of vaccination in the past—for instance, for protecting children from various diseases—we had an increasing number of parents who did what economists call "free riding": they basically assumed that if everyone else's child is vaccinated, they will not have to expose their child to whatever risk is entailed through vaccination; their child will still be protected. So, let's start with asking, How far are we willing to go in the prevention period to see that everybody takes the limited risk and participates? Because obviously, if more and more people bow out, the whole system is going to fall apart.

**ALAN KRAUT:** I think public shame went out with the Puritans. I don't think we're going to put people in stocks. But I think in the case of school boards and so on, there will be less tolerance on the part of those officials who are most directly involved. In other words, those who don't want to have the vaccination, parents who don't want to have their children vaccinated, are going to be subjected to greatly increased public pressure, possibly social ostracism, possibly simply exclusion from the public discourse. What other measure can one adopt? In short, in crisis period, and we're talking about something that's really crisis management, the traditional level of individualism probably isn't going to be as tolerable as it was in a calmer period.

**FITZHUGH MULLAN:** I would be for very strenuous laws and means to prosecute any campaign of vaccination. We do that essentially with children. There are many loopholes; states treat it a little bit differently. We use schools as the hammer, actually, because kids can't go to school if their vaccine card isn't up to date. There are exclusions for religious and other reasons. Now with this scenario, we're moving in a different time frame—and with the whole population, not just kids. But I would both write laws and enforce laws that were very exacting in terms of 100 percent vaccination, if that was what was the target of mass vaccination.

**AK:** I would, too. I think in the redefined kind of warfare that we're talking about, we can't avoid the notion that the civilians in the society are also subject to a discipline usually reserved to the military.

**AE:** As bin Laden keeps reminding us.

**AK:** As bin Laden keeps reminding us. And it's sad but it's true. In the case of those in uniform, their bodies belong to the United States Army or the United States Navy. Certain things can be done to them, and they can be exposed to certain dangers to which we wouldn't ordinarily expose a civilian population. But I think in this redefined kind of world, and redefined kind of situation, where there is a palpable threat, I agree with Fitz. I think there's a very good argument to be made to compel people to comply with a vaccination in a way that we ordinarily wouldn't, given our culture, given our society, and given our mores.

**RICHARD RIEGELMAN:** I think that the issue of vaccination revolves very much around what is the risk of the vaccination itself, as well as the risk of having an epidemic. But the risk of the old vaccine was considered to be quite high. The hope is that the new technologies for developing vaccines will actually reduce very substantially the risk; side effects are expected to be far less severe. But these new vaccines will be put into effect without any of the standard testing, so we are flying by the seat of our pants in terms of how safe these vaccines are going to be.

## WHERE TO DRAW THE LINE?

**AE:** All right, so now we've had the attack, and let's assume the terrorists used smallpox. So now we get the scenario, and instead of doing what some say is very harsh and very un-American—locking up many citizens and using at least nonviolent means to keep them there—we have the suggestion from D. A. Henderson [the original director of the Office of Public Health Preparedness in the Department of Health and Human Services, an office created in October 2001] that we should encourage people to stay home. It would be a system of voluntary domestic quarantining.

**AK:** Well, I haven't seen the full proposal, but it sounds rather unrealistic that people are going to accept voluntarily that kind of a societal lockdown, that families won't try to see extended members of the family and friends, and so on. It really doesn't sound like a very practical way to do it.

**FM:** My sense is, not having talked to him [Henderson] about it, that there may be ways to abate or buffer the epidemic, short of a formal, physical quarantine of hundreds of thousands of people. This is something that you walk back to after you examine the alternative, that is, the full formal lockdown of hundreds of thousands of people. I have not engaged in that war game entirely, but people are doing that. And to the extent that I have visited that scenario, it's a hard one to envision. I think it's not one we should duck, and at least in its broad outlines it makes more epidemiologic sense. But when you talk about quarantining Washington, D.C., or Topeka, Kansas, the implications are far beyond anything we've ever experienced. And I would like personally to see that walked through as to how that would work.

**AE:** Henderson's argument is, first of all, as far as extended family is concerned, I think he would say once we explain to people that if you go to visit your grandmother, you're killing her, they may want to refrain from visiting her for seventeen days. And what concerned me initially when I heard that is if I am infected and stay home, I'm going to infect my family who are healthy at that moment, and surely I will not want to do that. I'd rather go voluntarily to the place of quarantining. But it was explained to me that Henderson would suggest that you immediately vaccinate the other members of the families and you have this two-day window in which you can do that. I think there's a little more reality to it than there seems at first—other than that there's one catch, which in my judgment is not surmountable. This plan assumes a very high compliance rate. It assumes that not only will all people who have the symptoms then voluntarily stay home, be sure that nobody visits them, and have no member of the family go out—which is a hell of an assumption, as we know from compliance in practically any other medical intervention—but, worse, it assumes that a very high percentage of the people will recognize the symptoms correctly, including in our less educated population.

**AK:** Using history as an example, if we take a look at the polio epidemic in 1916, and we take a look at how families reacted that were quarantined, that had a child quarantined, how neighboring families attempted to send their children out of town and to evade quarantine signs that were hung in apartment buildings in Philadelphia and in New York, there's not a really good record on Americans complying. This individual ethic, which is such an important part of the American consciousness, of the American ethos, really works against expecting that kind of compliance. The reporting and the compliance will not be readily forthcoming.

**AE:** So now we discovered that after we tried voluntary quarantining for one week, the cost in human life was immense. We are now in a new city, and we have an early warning system that tells us daily about new infections. And we are now examining this harsh option of quarantining. Now, we do not need in this case to quarantine the whole family because we want to quarantine only those people who have early indications of the illness and we catch them, we assume, before the contagious stage. We don't want to quarantine the whole city, we just want to ask people who have the symptoms to join us at the most luxurious beach resort we can find, around which we are going to throw a ten-foot wall, reinforced by guards with nonviolent means of stopping people who want to leave.

**FM:** I don't think that's a likely scenario. I want to step back. I think we're misreading a little bit the public health management of scenario one, the initial scenario where amidst a population of hundreds of thousands, a number of thousand have been exposed—you just aren't quite sure who, or you're sure who's exposed but not to what extent. If we're talking smallpox and we're talking current vaccine supplies, the ring notion was that you vaccinate everybody who was in contact or is likely to be in contact with an infected person, and that basically provides protection, containment, exhaustion, or the extinction of that particular mini-epidemic. The problem with multiple individuals in a city is you can't ring them very easily. They are in a hundred thousand different places amid a population of a million. Then you talk about mass vaccination, and that is plausible. You can mass vaccinate everybody in that city very rapidly. It would be better if our public health structure was in better shape to do it, but depending upon the circumstance, that's quite plausible.

With smallpox the problem is when you run out of vaccine and you've still got cases in two or three other cities. Then you are in a situation where you now have lost your defense, your vaccine, and then quarantine becomes your only way to limit it. Then you come to the question, now perhaps robbed of any immunologic defense, as in vaccine, how do you contain the epidemic? And that gets to be a very difficult scenario in terms of people wanting to flee the area in particular, and the necessity to keep them there until either the epidemic runs its course or, with what vaccine you have available, you have contained it as well as you can. I think the big problem there is you're going to have people who are not sick, don't think they've been exposed, or maybe even think they've been exposed but don't want to stick around to find out, who are anxious to get out—out of the area, out of the country—and that's when I think you'll have enormous problems containing people.

**AE:** Let's hold it just for one second because I want to clarify the scenario. First of all, I don't know that everybody knows that we don't have endless vaccines ready. And there are some questions about how effective those vaccines we do have are because they've been sitting there since the 1970s. Is that a fair question?

**FM:** Yes.

**AE:** And how long will it take us to make another hundred million? Over twelve months?

**AK:** I think the plan calls for delivery within months. And I think that the key is that this strategy avoids some of these harsh decisions we have been discussing because it prepares us, if there is an outbreak, to quickly implement this kind of a strategy.

**AE:** You see, I salute and celebrate your tender hearts, in that you keep saying, "That's hard; I don't want to go there." But it's my job to take you there. So, let's go back to Fitz's scenario. We expend our vaccines and we now have some outbreaks in the city and we have zero left in the vault. And I am still not quite clear why we have to quarantine people who have no sign of illness. We are in the phase where they are not yet contagious, but they have the severe flu-warning symptoms. Why do we have to take anybody else but these people and invite them to our beach?

**FM:** Those people are clearly sick. What you have, however, is a twelve- to seventeen-day latent period, during which time people who may be infected show no symptoms.

**AE:** But during this period they are not contagious. So say that person who has been exposed and has no symptoms runs from Chicago to

Philadelphia. And now if she shows symptoms in Philadelphia, she'll be invited from there to go to the beach. So why do we want to stop people who have no symptoms? Why is it not enough to quarantine those who have symptoms in the precontagious stage?

**FM:** As a hypothetical matter I think that makes reasonable sense. The question of when symptoms are identified and who reports them and whether there is forthcomingness on the part of individuals, that becomes, I think, very difficult. I mean, hypothetically, if you had a point where they go from being noninfectious to being infectious or nonsymptomatic to being symptomatic infectious, you'd need to move them to the Etzioni Hilton at that point, that would be convenient. Theoretically, that would make sense. I think practically, that would be very difficult.

**AK:** Essentially, it's an issue of reporting.

## DRASTIC TIMES, DRASTIC MEASURES

**AE:** Let's move to the ultimate now. When our vaccine ring no longer exists, we'll have to throw walls around cities so we do not have to go into sorting and reporting. Should we let the plague get out of control in order not to do that?

**AK:** My answer would be no. You can't let the plague get out of control. At that point, the broader public health of the society, the country, the very survival of the society is at stake, and there is a good argument to be made for imposing laws and using force if necessary. The strictest quarantine possible must be imposed.

**AE:** You are not agreeing?

**FM:** I quickly confess to running out of tactical and ethical insight. I mean this is medieval. I mean that was the notion during those times, and our terminology recently slipped to plague rather than smallpox. This was the way plague was handled. People were confined to this town or that area. The vector plague was not understood then, but people knew they were going to die—and large numbers of people as well—because they were being forced to stay where it was until it effectively burned itself out. And whole towns in some cases in the fourteenth century expired that way. Trying to do that with Chicago today tests the limits of anything I can conceive of.

**RR:** I think coercion, in the communitarian terminology, is most effective at the beginning. If uniformly and quickly implemented, it can be implemented on the smallest possible scale. So, get in there and get in there quick and use coercion, but use it quickly and modestly.

**AE:** Now let's change direction a little, and let's talk about the agencies and the players who could participate and what difference it makes. Who does the early warning? Who does the education? Who does the quarantining? And one place maybe to start is to say that maybe this is the time to make Americans less individualistic.

**AK:** Well that's easy to say, hard to do. You can change all kinds of things about the situation and the society, but changing the fundamental values of Americans—values with which they've been educated and raised and taught because of a democratic heritage—that's hard to do. Their individualism is the bedrock of their national character. Reeducation sounds far and away like the most humane and proper way to do it. But how could you do something like that when we have difficulty with Americans accepting that there might be limits on who could get a kidney dialysis and accepting that kind of a triage situation? How much more difficult would it be in an atmosphere of panic to get people to accept the sacrifice of their freedom of choice voluntarily?

**FM:** I would disagree with that. Understanding Alan's premises, I would concur on his historical interpretation. We talk about the closing of the frontier, which was an important historical concept, speaking of the Western frontier. But the notion that we were an island nation and we were essentially protected, naturally quarantined from malevolent forces in the world—I think September 11, etcetera, etcetera, is going to bring that notion of frontier to a close for many of us who thought otherwise. It seems to me that an important adaptive feature of America in the future is going to have to be a sense of being part of the globe and being part of a community that has to defend itself. But this has to be more of a collective enterprise. The specter of biological disaster is like the Blitz in World War II in London. Nationwide, we're going to have to pull together. I don't think we can be the same country after this.

**AE:** I just want to take one second and switch my hat from just provoking and prodding to being a communitarian witness. First of all, the good news is, and I think I'm correct and certainly not alone, in reading American history, there has always been a tension between the Lockean notion of rights and individualism and the kind of communitarian, civic republican virtues and civility commitments. The very fact that the preamble talks about how we came together to form a more perfect union seems to be speaking to the other half of that struggle. But to go back to what happened after 9/11, that may change one more time. But at the moment, a lot of public opinion polls show a really dramatic shift in the willingness to care for each other, from blood donations to volunteering, and to trust our institutions and such. Now I'm not willing to predict how long it's going to last, but I don't want to leave it that we have no communitarian bone in our body.

**AK:** We do have a communitarian bone in our body during wartime and crisis situations, but one has to observe that those tend to be fairly short-term situations and they've always been somewhat limited before. And there have been violations of that communitarian spirit, whether we're talking about draft dodging or we're talking about buying oneself out of the service during the Civil War. In the aftermath of September 11 there is a lot of display of heartfelt communitarian spirit and spirit of cooperation and self-sacrifice, but I'm wondering in a sustained kind of conflict how long that lasts on a broad level. And faced with the kind of scenarios that we've been talking about, to what extent do people revert?

**RR:** Not only that, I think that the individualism has been expressed in institutional individualism, where everybody is competing and nobody's cooperating. And that's private-public; that's state, federal, and local; that's public health, hospitals, and physicians. If there's going to be a community, it's not just the individual behavior, it's institutional behavior that I think we need to focus on.

## A BETTER FUTURE?

**AE:** It's time now to let our imaginations really roam free. Can we use the threat of bioterrorism, and the need to deal with it, to build a better society and one in which there'll be more attention paid to public health?

**AK:** I would say yes. I would say that every war that the United States has ever fought has had indirect dividends in terms of what we've done medically, what we've done organizationally, creating new relationships between different parts of the government, different relationships between federal and state governments. And this current crisis is no exception. I think we're going to see out of this terrible situation, this national crisis, a set of new relationships. Some of it may have to do with different funding for the CDC, different balance of funding between different branches of the Public Health Service. A lot of it, I suspect, will have to do with the coordination between federal, state, and local. I think the kinds of chaos that we've been seeing, that we've been witnessing on almost a daily basis over who has jurisdiction over what and who ought to go to the microphone and who ought to be communicating with the White House—that's a lesson from a lack of preparedness and a lack of sound organizational practice. It probably will be corrected out of what we're seeing.

**RR:** I think we're going to see things that we knew we should have done for years now be done. This morning's news says that influenza has to be prevented now because it looks like anthrax. We're going to have the best immunization against influenza that we've ever had, and that's just hopefully the beginning. We're going to be applying our technology to put vaccines on the map. AIDS vaccines were never at the top of anybody's financing stream until recently, and the technology has to be applied, we have to use the most modern technology. We have had no surveillance system that comprehensibly looks for disease. We're going to have that now because we need it and hopefully it will have all kinds of spin-off effects that will improve our ability to monitor, detect, and rapidly react to new problems.

**FM:** I think Alan's point is a very good one, that crisis makes for opportunity. And both realigning what you have and creating new things will come out of this crisis as it's come out of others. So, I don't feel fatalistic about that. There are two specific things that occur to me. One is that as we consider massive new funding in this area, there is an instinct to buy vaccines and to stockpile immediate antibioterror implements—drugs, vaccines, etcetera. And that is as it should be. But if we don't invest at the same time in the infrastructure, the personnel, the communications capabilities, we will have lost that opportunity. So, to take this from the theoretical to the real, the design of the legislation and the funding of the legislation that we'll see coming forth very quickly here needs to take that into account. And there is an agenda ready to be funded. This is not a field that has gone unexamined. And the second thing is that I would hope that young people in the health sciences—in medicine and nursing, in public health, etcetera—think about their careers and weather the challenges, the tribulations, and the excitement of working in the public domain as doctors, nurses, and public health professionals more focused on and trained in these kinds of community-wide, population-wide, collectivist and communitarian issues. I hope many more will elect those kinds of careers.

**AE:** Well this is extremely helpful. So I'm taking away from this that we better prevent, and better be prepared before we are hit, and that we are much better off to the extent that we can rely on education. But we have no illusions that that will suffice, and we would, beyond that, if push comes to shove, rely on having vaccinations ready so that we can surround those who are ill with vaccination to prevent its spread. And we would resort to other voluntary means, which include putting pressures on those people who are not willing to line up and be vaccinated because they are individualistic or free riders or fearful. But we also realize that we may have to engage in full-blown quarantining. And, finally and maybe most importantly, out of these terrible tragedies some good may arise if we use this challenge to reinstitutionalize this— temporary, I grant—very community-minded spirit.

I also take one more thing away from this: that we can have a reasoned dialogue without hardball. Without interrupting each other or attacking each other, we had what I thought was an excellent, productive conversation. Dr. Kraut, Dr. Riegelman, Dr. Mullan—thank you very, very much for participating in this communitarian dialogue.

## NOTE

This chapter was originally published in *The Responsive Community* 12, no. 2 (spring 2002): 59–70.

# A Just War?

# 14

# WHAT WE'RE FIGHTING FOR: A LETTER FROM AMERICA

*The following letter was drafted in February 2002 under the auspices of the Institute for American Values, a New York think tank devoted to contributing intellectually to the renewal of marriage and family life and the sources of character and citizenship. The letter's seven primary authors were Enola Aird, affiliate scholar of the institute; David Blankenhorn, president of the institute; Jean Bethke Elshtain, the Laura Spelman Rockefeller Professor of Social and Political Ethics at the University of Chicago; Francis Fukuyama, Bernard Schwartz Professor of International Political Studies at Johns Hopkins University; Robert P. George, McCormick Professor of Jurisprudence and professor of politics at Princeton University; Mary Ann Glendon, the Learned Hand Professor of Law at Harvard University; and James Q. Wilson, emeritus professor of management and public policy at the University of California, Los Angeles.*

**A**t times it becomes necessary for a nation to defend itself through force of arms. Because war is a grave matter, involving the sacrifice and taking of precious human life, conscience demands that those who would wage the war state clearly the moral reasoning behind their actions, in order to make plain to one another, and to the world community, the principles they are defending.

We affirm five fundamental truths that pertain to all people without distinction:

1. All human beings are born free and equal in dignity and rights.[1]
2. The basic subject of society is the human person, and the legitimate role of government is to protect and help to foster the conditions for human flourishing.[2]
3. Human beings naturally desire to seek the truth about life's purpose and ultimate ends.[3]
4. Freedom of conscience and religious freedom are inviolable rights of the human person.[4]
5. Killing in the name of God is contrary to faith in God and is the greatest betrayal of the universality of religious faith.[5]

We fight to defend ourselves and to defend these universal principles.


## WHAT ARE AMERICAN VALUES?

Since September 11, millions of Americans have asked themselves and one another, why? Why are we the targets of these hateful attacks? Why do those who would kill us, want to kill us?

We recognize that at times our nation has acted with arrogance and ignorance toward other societies. At times our nation has pursued misguided and unjust policies. Too often we as a nation have failed to live up to our ideals. We cannot urge other societies to abide by moral principles without simultaneously admitting our own society's failure at times to abide by those same principles. We are united in our conviction—and are confident that all people of goodwill in the world will agree—that no appeal to the merits or demerits of specific foreign policies can ever justify, or even purport to make sense of, the mass slaughter of innocent persons.

Moreover, in a democracy such as ours, in which government derives its power from the consent of the governed, policy stems at least partly from culture, from the values and priorities of the society as a whole. Though we do not claim to possess full knowledge of the motivations of our attackers and their sympathizers, what we do know suggests that their grievances extend far beyond any one policy, or set of policies. After all, the killers of September 11 issued no particular demands; in this sense, at least, the killing was done for its own sake. The leader of al-Qaeda described the "blessed strikes" of September 11 as blows against America, "the head of world infidelity."[6] Clearly, then, our attackers despise not just our government, but our overall society, our entire way of living. Fundamentally, their grievance concerns not only what our leaders do, but also *who we are.*

So who are we? What do we value? For many people, including many Americans and a number of signatories to this letter, some values sometimes seen in America are unattractive and harmful. Consumerism as a way of life. The notion of freedom as no rules. The notion of the individual as self-made and utterly sovereign, owing little to others or to society. The weakening of marriage and family life. Plus an enormous entertainment and communications apparatus that relentlessly glorifies such ideas and beams them, whether they are welcome or not, into nearly every corner of the globe.

One major task facing us as Americans, important prior to September 11, is facing honestly these unattractive aspects of our society and doing all we can to change them for the better. We pledge ourselves to this effort.

At the same time, other American values—what we view as our founding ideals, and those that most define our way of life—are quite different from these, and they are much more attractive, not only to Americans, but to people everywhere in the world. Let us briefly mention four of them.[7]

The first is the conviction that all persons possess innate human dignity as a birthright, and that consequently each person must always be treated as an end rather than used as a means. The founders of the United States, drawing upon the natural law tradition as well as upon the fundamental religious claim that all persons are created in the image of God, affirmed as "self-evident" the idea that all persons possess equal dignity. The clearest political expression of a belief in transcendent human dignity is democracy. In the United States in recent generations, among the clearest cultural expressions of this idea has been the affirmation of the equal dignity of men and women, and of all persons regardless of race or color.

Second, and following closely from the first, is the conviction that universal moral truths (what our nation's founders called "laws of Nature and of Nature's God") exist and are accessible to all people. Some of the most eloquent expressions of our reliance upon these truths are found in our Declaration of Independence, George Washington's Farewell Address, Abraham Lincoln's Gettysburg Address and Second Inaugural Address, and Dr. Martin Luther King Jr.'s Letter from the Birmingham Jail.

The third is the conviction that, because our individual and collective access to truth is imperfect, most disagreements about values call for civility, openness to other views, and reasonable argument in pursuit of truth.

The fourth is freedom of conscience and freedom of religion. These intrinsically connected freedoms are widely recognized, in our own country and elsewhere, as a reflection of basic human dignity and as a precondition for other individual freedoms.[8]

To us, what is most striking about these values is that they apply to all persons without distinction, and cannot be used to exclude anyone from recognition and respect based on the particularities of race, language, memory, or religion. That's why anyone, in principle, can become an American. And in fact, anyone does. People from everywhere in the world come to our country with what a statue in New York's harbor calls a yearning to breathe free, and soon enough, they are Americans. Historically, no other nation has forged its core identity—its constitution and other founding documents, as well as its basic self-understanding—so directly and explicitly on the basis of universal human values. To us, no other fact about this country is more important.

Some people assert that these values are not universal at all, but instead derive particularly from Western, largely Christian civilization. They argue that to conceive of these values as universal is to deny the distinctiveness of other cultures.[9] We disagree. We recognize our own civilization's achievements, but we believe that all people are created equal. We believe in the universal possibility and desirability of human freedom. We believe that certain basic moral truths are recognizable everywhere in the world. We agree with the international group of distinguished philosophers who in the late 1940s helped to shape the United Nations Universal Declaration of Human Rights, and who concluded that a few fundamental moral ideas are so widespread that they "may be viewed as implicit in man's nature as a member of society."[10] In hope, and on the evidence, we agree with Dr. Martin Luther King Jr. that the arc of the moral universe is long, but it bends toward justice, not just for the few, or the lucky, but for all people.[11]

Looking at our own society, we acknowledge again the all too frequent gaps between our ideals and our conduct. But as Americans in a time of war and global crisis, we are also suggesting that the *best* of what we too casually call "American values" do not belong only to America, but are in fact the shared inheritance of humankind, and therefore a possible basis of hope for a world community based on peace and justice.

## WHAT ABOUT GOD?

Since September 11, millions of Americans have asked themselves and one another, what about God? Crises of this magnitude force us to think anew about first principles. When we contemplate the horror of what has occurred, and the danger of what is likely to come, many of us ask: Is religious faith part of the solution or part of the problem?

The signatories to this letter come from diverse religious and moral traditions, including secular traditions. We are united in our belief that invoking God's authority to kill or maim human beings is immoral and is contrary to faith in God. Many of us believe that we are under God's judgment. None of us believe that God ever instructs some of us to kill or conquer others of us. Indeed, such an attitude, whether it is called "holy war" or "crusade," not only violates basic principles of justice, but is in fact a negation of religious faith, since it turns God into an idol to be used for man's own purposes.[12] Our own nation was once engaged in a great civil war, in which each side presumed God's aid against the other. In his Second Inaugural Address in 1865, the sixteenth president of the United States, Abraham Lincoln, put it simply: "The Almighty has his own purposes."

Those who attacked us on September 11 openly proclaim that they are engaged in holy war. Many who support or sympathize with the attackers also invoke God's name and seem to embrace the rationale of holy war. But to recognize the disaster of this way of thinking, we as

Americans need only to remember our own, and Western, history. Christian religious wars and Christian sectarian violence tore apart Europe for the better part of a century. In the United States, we are no strangers to those who would murder at least in part in the name of their religious faith. When it comes to this particular evil, no civilization is spotless and no religious tradition is spotless.[13]

The human person has a basic drive to question in order to know. Evaluating, choosing, and having reasons for what we value and love are characteristically human activities.[14] Part of this intrinsic desire to know concerns why we are born and what will happen when we die, which leads us to seek the truth about ultimate ends, including, for many people, the question of God. Some of the signatories to this letter believe that human beings are by nature "religious" in the sense that everyone, including those who do not believe in God and do not participate in organized religion, makes choices about what is important and reflects on ultimate values. All of the signatories to this letter recognize that, across the world, religious faith and religious institutions are important bases of civil society, often producing results for society that are beneficial and healing, at times producing results that are divisive and violent.

So how can governments and societal leaders best respond to these fundamental human and social realities? One response is to outlaw or repress religion. Another possible response is to embrace an ideological secularism:[15] a strong societal skepticism or hostility regarding religion, based on the premise that religion itself, and especially any *public* expression of religious conviction, is inherently problematic. A third possible response is to embrace theocracy: the belief that one religion, presumably the one *true* religion, should be effectively mandatory for all members of society and therefore should receive complete or significant state sponsorship and support.

We disagree with each of these responses. Legal repression radically violates civil and religious freedom and is incompatible with democratic civil society. Although ideological secularism may have increased in our society in recent generations, we disagree with it because it would deny the public legitimacy of an important part of civil society as well as seek to suppress or deny the existence of what is at least arguably an important dimension of personhood itself.[16] Although theocracy has been present in Western (though not U.S.) history, we disagree with it for

both social and theological reasons. Socially, governmental establishment of a particular religion can conflict with the principle of religious
freedom, a fundamental human right. In addition, government control
of religion can cause or exacerbate religious conflicts and, perhaps even
more importantly, can threaten the vitality and authenticity of religious
institutions. Theologically, even for those who are firmly convinced of
the truth of their faith, the coercion of others in matters of religious conscience is ultimately a violation of religion itself, since it robs those other
persons of the right to respond freely and in dignity to the Creator's in-
vitation.

At its best, the United States seeks to be a society in which faith and
freedom can go together, each elevating the other. We have a secular
state—our government officials are not simultaneously religious
officials—but we are by far the Western world's most religious society.
We are a nation that deeply respects religious freedom and diversity, including the rights of nonbelievers, but one whose citizens recite a
Pledge of Allegiance to "one nation, under God," and one that proclaims
in many of its courtrooms and inscribes on each of its coins the motto,
"In God We Trust." Politically, our separation of church and state seeks
to keep politics within its proper sphere, in part by limiting the state's
power to control religion, and in part by causing government itself to
draw legitimacy from, and operate under, a larger moral canopy that is
not of its own making.[17] Spiritually, our separation of church and state
permits religion to *be* religion, by detaching it from the coercive power
of government. In short, we seek to separate church and state for the
protection and proper vitality of both.[18]

For Americans of religious faith, the challenge of embracing religious
truth *and* religious freedom has often been difficult. The matter, moreover, is never settled. Ours is a social and constitutional arrangement
that almost by definition requires constant deliberation, debate, adjust-
ment, and compromise. It is also helped by, and helps to produce, a certain character or temperament, such that religious believers who
strongly embrace the truth of their faith also, not as a compromise with
that truth but as an aspect of it, respect those who take a different path.

What will help to reduce religiously based mistrust, hatred, and violence in the twenty-first century? There are many important answers
to this question, of course, but here, we hope, is one: deepening and

renewing our appreciation of religion by recognizing religious freedom as a fundamental right of all people in every nation.

## A JUST WAR?

We recognize that all war is terrible, representative finally of human political failure. We also know that the line separating good and evil does
not run between one society and another, much less between one religion and another; ultimately, that line runs through the middle of every
human heart.[19] Finally, those of us—Jews, Christians, Muslims, and
others—who are people of faith recognize our responsibility, stated in
our holy scriptures, to love mercy and to do all in our power to prevent
war and live in peace.

Yet reason and careful moral reflection also teach us that there are
times when the first and most important reply to evil is to stop it. There
are times when waging war is not only morally permitted, but morally
necessary, as a response to calamitous acts of violence, hatred, and injustice. This is one of those times.

The idea of a "just war" is broadly based, with roots in many of the
world's diverse religious and secular moral traditions.[20] Jewish, Christian, and Muslim teachings, for example, all contain serious reflections
on the definition of a just war. To be sure, some people, often in the
name of realism, insist that war is essentially a realm of self-interest and
necessity, making most attempts at moral analysis irrelevant.[21] We
disagree.[22] Moral inarticulacy in the face of war is itself a moral stance—
one that rejects the possibility of reason, accepts normlessness in international affairs, and capitulates to cynicism. To seek to apply objective
moral reasoning to war is to defend the possibility of civil society and a
world community based on justice.

The principles of just war teach us that wars of aggression and ag-
grandizement are never acceptable. Wars may not legitimately be
fought for national glory, to avenge past wrongs, for territorial gain, or
for any other nondefensive purpose.

The primary moral justification for war is to protect the innocent from
certain harm. Augustine, whose early fifth-century book *The City of
God* is a seminal contribution to just war thinking, argues (echoing

Socrates)[23] that it is better for the Christian as an individual to suffer harm rather than to commit it. But is the morally responsible person also required, or even permitted, to make for *other* innocent persons a commitment to non-self-defense? For Augustine, and for the broader just war tradition, the answer is no. If one has compelling evidence that innocent people who are in no position to protect themselves will be grievously harmed unless coercive force is used to stop an aggressor, then the moral principle of love of neighbor calls us to the use of force.

Wars may not legitimately be fought against dangers that are small, questionable, or of uncertain consequence, or against dangers that might plausibly be mitigated solely through negotiation, appeals to reason, persuasion from third parties, or other nonviolent means.[24] But if the danger to innocent life is real and certain, and especially if the aggressor is motivated by implacable hostility—if the end he seeks is not your willingness to negotiate or comply, but rather your destruction—then a resort to proportionate force is morally justified.

A just war can only be fought by a legitimate authority with responsibility for public order. Violence that is freelance, opportunistic, or individualistic is never morally acceptable.[25] A just war can only be waged against persons who are combatants. Just war authorities from across history and around the world—whether they be Muslim, Jewish, Christian, from other faith traditions, or secular—consistently teach us that noncombatants are immune from deliberate attack. Thus, killing civilians for revenge, or even as a means of deterring aggression from people who sympathize with them, is morally wrong. Although in some circumstances, and within strict limits, it can be morally justifiable to undertake military actions that may result in the unintended but foreseeable death or injury of some noncombatants, it is not morally acceptable to make the killing of noncombatants the operational objective of a military action.

These and other just war principles teach us that, whenever human beings contemplate or wage war, it is both possible and necessary to affirm the sanctity of human life and embrace the principle of equal human dignity.[26] These principles strive to preserve and reflect, even in the tragic activity of war, the fundamental moral truth that "others"— those who are strangers to us, those who differ from us in race or language, those whose religions we may believe to be untrue—have the same right to life that we do, and the same human dignity and human rights that we do.

On September 11, 2001, a group of individuals deliberately attacked the United States, using highjacked airplanes as weapons with which to kill in less than two hours over 3,000 of our citizens in New York City, southwestern Pennsylvania, and Washington, D.C.[27] Overwhelmingly, those who died on September 11 were civilians, not combatants, and were not known at all, except as Americans, by those who killed them. Those who died on the morning of September 11 were killed unlawfully, wantonly, and with premeditated malice—a kind of killing that, in the name of precision, can only be described as murder. Those murdered included people from all races, many ethnicities, most major religions. They included dishwashers and corporate executives.

The individuals who committed these acts of war did not act alone, or without support, or for unknown reasons. They were members of an international Islamicist network, active in as many as forty countries, now known to the world as al-Qaeda. This group, in turn, constitutes but one arm of a larger radical Islamicist movement, growing for decades and in some instances tolerated and even supported by governments, that openly professes its desire and increasingly demonstrates its ability to use murder to advance its objectives.[28]

We use the terms "Islam" and "Islamic" to refer to one of the world's great religions, with about 1.2 billion adherents, including several million U.S. citizens, some of whom were murdered on September 11. It ought to go without saying—but we say it here once, clearly—that the great majority of the world's Muslims, guided in large measure by the teachings of the Qur'an, are decent, faithful, and peaceful. We use the terms "Islamicism" and "radical Islamicist" to refer to the violent, extremist, and radically intolerant religious–political movement that now threatens the world, including the Muslim world.

This radical, violent movement opposes not only certain U.S. and Western policies—some signatories to this letter also oppose some of those policies—but also a foundational principle of the modern world, religious tolerance, as well as those fundamental human rights, in particular freedom of conscience and religion, that are enshrined in the United Nations Universal Declaration of Human Rights, and that must be the basis of any civilization oriented to human flourishing, justice, and peace.

This extremist movement claims to speak for Islam, but betrays fundamental Islamic principles. Islam sets its face *against* moral atrocities. For example, reflecting the teaching of the Qur'an and the example of the Prophet, Muslim scholars through the centuries have taught that struggle in the path of God (i.e., jihad) forbids the deliberate killing of noncombatants, and requires that military action be undertaken only at the behest of legitimate public authorities.[29] They remind us forcefully that Islam, no less than Christianity, Judaism, and other religions, is threatened and potentially degraded by these profaners who invoke God's name to kill indiscriminately.[30]

We recognize that movements claiming the mantle of religion also have complex political, social, and demographic dimensions, to which due attention must be paid. At the same time, philosophy matters, and the animating philosophy of this radical Islamicist movement, in its contempt for human life and by viewing the world as a life-and-death struggle between believers and unbelievers (whether non-radical Muslims, Jews, Christians, Hindus, or others), clearly denies the equal dignity of all persons; in doing so, it betrays religion and rejects the very foundation of civilized life and the possibility of peace among nations.

Most seriously of all, the mass murders of September 11 demonstrated, arguably for the first time, that this movement now possesses not only the openly stated desire, but also the capacity and expertise—including possible access to, and willingness to use, chemical, biological, and nuclear weapons—to wreak massive, horrific devastation on its intended targets.[31] Those who slaughtered more than 3,000 persons on September 11 and who, by their own admission, want nothing more than to do it again, constitute a clear and present danger to all people of good will everywhere in the world, not just the United States. Such acts are a pure example of naked aggression against innocent human life, a world-threatening evil that clearly requires the use of force to remove it.

Organized killers with global reach now threaten all of us. In the name of universal human morality, and fully conscious of the restrictions and requirements of a just war, we support our government's, and our society's, decision to use force of arms against them.

## CONCLUSION

We pledge to do all we can to guard against the harmful temptations—especially those of arrogance and jingoism—to which nations at war so often seem to yield. At the same time, with one voice we say solemnly that it is crucial for our nation and its allies to win this war. We fight to defend ourselves, but we also believe that we fight to defend those universal principles of human rights and human dignity that are the best hope for humankind.

One day, this war will end. When it does—and in some respects even before it ends—the great task of conciliation awaits us. We hope that this war, by stopping an unmitigated global evil, can increase the possibility of a world community based on justice. But we know that only the peacemakers among us in every society can ensure that this war will not have been in vain. We wish especially to reach out to our brothers and sisters in Muslim societies. We say to you forthrightly: We are not enemies, but friends. We must not be enemies.[32] We have so much in common. There is so much that we must do together. Your human dignity, no less than ours—your rights and opportunities for a good life, no less than ours—are what we believe we're fighting for. We know that, for some of you, mistrust of us is high, and we know that we Americans are partly responsible for that mistrust. But we must not be enemies. In hope, we wish to join with you and all people of good will to build a just and lasting peace.

## ORIGINAL SIGNATORIES

Enola Aird, *director, The Motherhood Project, and member, Council on Civil Society;* John Atlas, *president, National Housing Institute, and executive director, Passaic County Legal Aid Society;* Jay Belsky, *professor and director, Institute for the Study of Children, Families and Social Issues, Birkbeck University of London;* David Blankenhorn, *president, Institute for American Values;* David Bosworth, *University of Washington;* R. Maurice Boyd, *minister, The City Church, New York;* Gerard V. Bradley, *professor of law, University of Notre Dame;* Margaret F. Brinig, *Edward A. Howry Distinguished Professor, University of Iowa College of Law;* Allan Carlson, *president, The Howard Center for Family, Religion, and Society;* Khalid Durán, *editor,* TransIslam Magazine; Paul

Ekman, *professor of psychology, University of California, San Francisco;* Jean Bethke Elshtain, *Laura Spelman Rockefeller Professor of Social and Political Ethics, University of Chicago Divinity School;* Amitai Etzioni, *University Professor, The George Washington University;* Hillel Fradkin, *president, Ethics and Public Policy Center;* Samuel G. Freedman, *professor, Columbia University Graduate School of Journalism;* Francis Fukuyama, *Bernard Schwartz Professor of International Political Economy, Johns Hopkins University;* William A. Galston, *professor, School of Public Affairs, University of Maryland, and director, Institute for Philosophy and Public Policy;* Claire Gaudiani, *senior research scholar, Yale Law School, and former president, Connecticut College;* Robert P. George, *McCormick Professor of Jurisprudence and Professor of Politics, Princeton University;* Neil Gilbert, *professor, School of Social Welfare, University of California, Berkeley;* Mary Ann Glendon, *Learned Hand Professor of Law, Harvard University Law School;* Norval D. Glenn, *Ashbel Smith Professor of Sociology and Stiles Professor of American Studies, University of Texas at Austin;* Os Guinness, *senior fellow, Trinity Forum;* David Gutmann, *professor emeritus of Psychiatry and Education, Northwestern University;* Kevin J. "Seamus" Hasson, *president, Becket Fund for Religious Liberty;* Sylvia Ann Hewlett, *chair, National Parenting Association;* James Davison Hunter, *William R. Kenan Jr., Professor of Sociology and Religious Studies and executive director, Center on Religion and Democracy, University of Virginia;* Samuel Huntington, *Albert J. Weatherhead, III, University Professor, Harvard University;* Byron Johnson, *director and distinguished senior fellow, Center for Research on Religion and Urban Civil Society, University of Pennsylvania;* James Turner Johnson, *professor, Department of Religion, Rutgers University;* John Kelsay, *Richard L. Rubenstein Professor of Religion, Florida State University;* Diane Knippers, *president, Institute on Religion and Democracy;* Thomas C. Kohler, *professor of law, Boston College Law School;* Glenn C. Loury, *professor of economics and director, Institute on Race and Social Division, Boston University;* Harvey C. Mansfield, *William R. Kenan Jr., professor of government, Harvard University;* Will Marshall, *president, Progressive Policy Institute;* Richard J. Mouw, *president, Fuller Theological Seminary;* Daniel Patrick Moynihan, *University Professor, Maxwell School of Citizenship and Public Affairs, Syracuse University;* John E. Murray Jr., *chancellor and professor of law, Duquesne University;* Michael Novak, *George Frederick Jewett Chair in Religion and Public Policy, American Enterprise Institute;* Rev. Val J. Peter, *executive director, Boys and Girls Town;* David Popenoe, *professor, sociology, codirector, National Marriage Project, Rutgers University;* Robert D. Putnam, *Peter and Isabel Malkin Professor of Public Policy at the Kennedy School of Government, Harvard University;* Gloria G. Rodriguez, *founder and president, AVANCE, Inc.;* Robert Royal, *president, Faith & Reason Institute;* Nina Shea, *director, Freedom House's Center for Religious Freedom;* Fred Siegel, *professor of history, The Cooper Union;* Theda Skocpol, *Victor S. Thomas Professor of Government and Sociology, Harvard University;* Katherine Shaw Spaht, *Jules and Frances Landry Professor of Law, Louisiana State University Law Center;* Max L. Stackhouse, *professor of Christian ethics and director, Project on Public Theology, Princeton Theological Seminary;* William Tell Jr., *The William and Karen Tell Foundation;* Maris A. Vinovskis, *Bentley Professor of History and Professor of Public Policy, University of Michigan;* Paul C. Vitz, *professor of psychology, New York University;* Michael Walzer, *professor, School of Social Science, Institute for Advanced Study;* George Weigel, *senior fellow, Ethics and Public Policy Center;* Charles Wilson, *director, Center for the Study of Southern Culture, University of Mississippi;* James Q. Wilson, *Collins Professor of Management and Public Policy Emeritus, University of California, Los Angeles;* John Witte Jr., *Jonas Robitscher Professor of Law and Ethics and director, Law and Religion Program, Emory University Law School;* Christopher Wolfe, *professor of political science, Marquette University;* Daniel Yankelovich, *president, Public Agenda.*

## NOTES

Subsequent notes added by the authors.

1. From the United Nations Universal Declaration of Human Rights, Article 1.

2. Council on Civil Society, *A Call to Civil Society: Why Democracy Needs Moral Truths* (New York: Institute for American Values, 1998), 16; Aristotle, *Politics* VII, 1-2.

3. Aristotle, *Metaphysics*, 1-1; John Paul II, *Fides et Ratio,* 25 (Vatican City, 1998).

4. United Nations Universal Declaration of Human Rights, Articles 18 and 19.

5. Bosphorus Declaration (Istanbul, Turkey, February 9, 1994); Berne Declaration (Wolfsberg/Zurich, Switzerland, November 26, 1992); and John Paul II, Papal Message for World Day of Peace, Articles 6 and 7 (Vatican City, January 1, 2002).

6. Walter Pincus, "New Videotape Features Pale Bin Laden; Al Qaeda Leader's Message Was Made Early December, U.S. Officials Say," *Washington Post*, December 27, 2001, A16.

7. See Council on Civil Society, *A Call to Civil Society.*

8. See John Witte Jr. and M. Christian Green, "The American Constitutional Experiment in Religious Human Rights: The Perennial Search for Principles,"

in Johan D. van der Vyver and John Witte Jr., eds., *Religious Human Rights in Global Perspective*, vol. 2 (The Hague: Martinus Nijhoff, 1996). See also Harold J. Berman, *Law and Revolution: The Formation of the Western Legal Tradition* (Cambridge, Mass.: Harvard University Press, 1983), and Michael J. Perry, *The Idea of Human Rights: Four Inquiries* (New York: Oxford University Press, 1998).

9. Some people make this point as a way of condemning those "other" cultures that are presumably too inferior, or too enthralled by false beliefs, to appreciate what we in this letter are calling universal human values; others make this point as a way of endorsing (usually *one* of) those cultures that are presumably indifferent to these values. We disagree with both versions of this point.

10. Richard McKeon, "The Philosophic Bases and Material Circumstances of the Rights of Man," in *Human Rights: Comments and Interpretations* (London: Wingate, 1949), 45.

11. Martin Luther King Jr., "Where Do We Go from Here?," in James M. Washington, ed., *The Essential Writings and Speeches of Martin Luther King, Jr.* (New York: HarperCollins, 1986), 245.

12. John Paul II, Papal Message for World Day of Peace, Article 6 (Vatican City, January 1, 2002).

13. Intra-Christian examples of holy war or crusade emerged with particular force in Europe during the seventeenth century. According to some scholars, the principle characteristics of holy war are that the cause for which the war is fought has a clear connection to religion (i.e., that the cause is "holy"); that the war is fought under the banner and with the presumption of divine authority and assistance (the Latin term used by eleventh-century Christian crusaders was "*Deus Volt*," or "God wills it"); that the warriors understand themselves to be godly, or "warrior saints"; that the war is prosecuted zealously and unsparingly since the enemy is presumed to be ungodly and therefore fundamentally "other," lacking the human dignity and rights of the godly; and, finally, that warriors who die in battle are favored by God as martyrs. Eventually, in Christianity, the development of just war doctrine, with its emphasis on moral universalism, largely called for the elimination of religion as a just cause for war. As early as the sixteenth century, some natural law theorists, such as Franciscus de Victoria and Francisco Suarez, were explicitly condemning the use of war to spread religion. "Difference in religion," Victoria wrote, "is not a cause of just war." See James Turner Johnson, *Ideology, Reason, and the Limitation of War: Religious and Secular Concepts 1200–1740* (Princeton, N.J.: Princeton University Press, 1975), 112–23, 154. See also Roland H. Bainton, *Christian Attitudes toward War and Peace: A Historical Survey and Critical Re-Evaluation* (Nashville, Tenn.: Abingdon, 1960), 148.

14. Council on Civil Society, *A Call to Civil Society*, 16. This theme is developed in Aristotle, *Metaphysics*, 1-1; see also Bernard J. Lonergan, *Insight: A Study of Human Understanding* (New York: Longmans, 1958).

15. We wish here to distinguish "secular" from "secularism." Secular, derived from the Latin term meaning "world" and suggesting "in the world," refers merely to functions that are separate from the church. Secularism, by contrast, is a philosophy, an "ism," a way of seeing the world based on rejection of religion or hostility to religion.

16. For this reason, advocates of secularism may underestimate the degree to which human societies, even in theory, can simply dispense with "religion." Moreover, they almost certainly miscalculate, even accepting many of their own premises, the social consequences of suppressing traditional religion. For if we understand religion to be values of ultimate concern, the twentieth century saw two world-threatening examples—Nazism in Germany and communism in the Soviet Union—of the emergence of secular religions, or what might be called replacement religions, each violently intent on eliminating its society's traditional religious faiths (in effect, its competitor faiths) and each, when in power, ruthlessly indifferent to human dignity and basic human rights.

17. As the leaders and scholars who produced the Williamsburg Charter put it in 1988, "The government acts as a safeguard, but not the source, of freedom for faiths, whereas the churches and synagogues act as a source, but not the safeguard, of faiths for freedom. . . . The result is neither a naked public square where all religion is excluded, nor a sacred public square with any religion established or semi-established. The result, rather, is a civil public square in which citizens of all religious faiths, or none, engage one another in the continuing democratic discourse." See James Davison Hunter and Os Guinness, eds., *Articles of Faith, Articles of Peace: The Religious Liberty Clauses and the American Public Philosophy* (Washington, D.C.: Brookings Institution, 1990), 140.

18. Council on Civil Society, *A Call to Civil Society*, 13.

19. See Alexander Solzhenitzyn, *The Gulag Archipelago*, vol. 1 (New York: Harper & Row, 1974), 168.

20. See Jean Bethke Elshtain, ed., *Just War Theory* (Oxford, U.K.: Blackwell, 1992); Elshtain, Stanley Hauerwas, and James Turner Johnson, Pew Forum on Religion and Public Life Conference on "Just War Tradition and the New War on Terrorism," at http://pewforum.org/events/1005; James Turner Johnson, *Ideology, Reason, and the Limitation of War, Just War Tradition and the Restraint of War: A Moral and Historical Inquiry* (Princeton, N.J.: Princeton University Press, 1981), *The Quest for Peace: Three Moral Traditions in Western Cultural History* (Princeton, N.J.: Princeton University Press, 1987),

and *Morality and Contemporary Warfare* (New Haven, Conn.: Yale University Press, 1999); James Turner Johnson and John Kelsay, eds., *Cross, Crescent, and Sword: The Justification and Limitation of War in Western and Islamic Tradition* (New York: Greenwood Press, 1990); Majid Khadduri, *War and Peace in the Law of Islam* (Baltimore, Md.: Johns Hopkins University Press, 1955); John Kelsay and James Turner Johnson, eds., *Just War and Jihad: Historical and Theoretical Perspectives on War and Peace in Western and Islamic Tradition* (New York: Greenwood Press, 1991); Terry Nardin, ed., *The Ethics of War and Peace: Religious and Secular Perspectives* (Princeton, N.J.: Princeton University Press, 1996); William V. O'Brien, *The Conduct of War and Limited War* (New York: Praeger, 1981); Rudolf Peters, *Jihad in Classical and Modern Islam* (Princeton, N.J.: Markus Wiener, 1996); Paul Ramsey, *Speak Up for Just War or Pacifism* (University Park: Pennsylvania State University Press, 1988); Michael Walzer, *Just and Unjust Wars* (New York: Basic Books, 1977); and Richard Wasserstrom, ed., *War and Morality* (Belmont, Calif.: Wadsworth, 1970).

21. The Latin axiom is, *Inter arma silent leges* (In times of war the law is silent). Classical exemplars of this perspective include Thucydides, Niccolò Machiavelli, and Thomas Hobbes; for a more recent treatment, see Kenneth Waltz, *Man, the State and War* (Princeton, N.J.: Princeton University Press, 1978). For a sensitive but critical survey of the contribution of this school of thought to international theory, see Jack Donnelly, *Realism and International Relations* (Cambridge, U.K.: Cambridge University Press, 2000).

22. Intellectual and moral approaches to war as a human phenomenon can generally be divided into four schools of thought. The first can be called realism: the belief that war is basically a matter of power, self-interest, necessity, and survival, thereby rendering abstract moral analysis largely beside the point. The second can be called holy war: the belief that God can authorize the coercion and killing of nonbelievers or that a particular secular ideology of ultimate concern can authorize the coercion and killing of nonbelievers. The third can be called pacifism: the belief that all war is intrinsically immoral. And the fourth is typically called just war: the belief that universal moral reasoning, or what some would call natural moral law, can and should be applied to the activity of war. The signatories to this letter largely disagree with the first school of thought. We unequivocally reject the second school of thought regardless of the form it takes or whether it springs from and purports to support our own society ("our side") or the side of those who wish us ill. Some of the signatories have much respect for the third school of thought (particularly its insistence that nonviolence does not mean retreat or passivity or declining to stand for justice; quite the opposite), even as we respectfully, and with some degree of fear

and trembling, differ from it. As a group, we seek largely to embrace and build on the fourth school of thought.

23. Socrates' judgment that it is better to suffer evil rather than to do it is conveyed to us by Plato in the *Apology* (32-c–32-e) and constitutes a key moment in moral philosophy.

24. Some people suggest that the "last resort" requirement of just war theory—in essence, the requirement to explore all other reasonable and plausible alternatives to the use of force—is not satisfied until the resort to arms has been approved by a recognized international body, such as the United Nations. This proposition is problematic. First, it is novel: historically, approval by an international body has not been viewed by just war theorists as a just cause requirement. Second, it is quite debatable whether an international body such as the United Nations is in a position to be the best final judge of when and under what conditions a particular resort to arms is justified or whether the attempt by that body to make and enforce such judgments would inevitably compromise its primary mission of humanitarian work. According to one observer, a former UN assistant secretary-general, transforming the United Nations into "a pale imitation of a state" in order to "manage the use of force" internationally "may well be a suicidal embrace." See Giandomenico Picco, "The U.N. and the Use of Force," *Foreign Affairs* 73 (1994): 15. See also Thomas G. Weis, David P. Forsythe, and Roger A. Coate, *United Nations and Changing World Politics* (Boulder, Colo.: Westview Press, 2001), 104–6; and John Gerard Ruggie, *The United Nations and the Collective Use of Force: Whither? Or Whether?* (New York: United Nations Association of the USA, 1996).

25. In just war theory, the main goal of the legitimate authority requirement is to prevent the anarchy of private warfare and warlords—an anarchy that exists today in some parts of the world and of which the attackers of September 11 are representative embodiments. The legitimate authority requirement does not, on the other hand, for several reasons, apply clearly or directly to wars of national independence or succession. First, these latter types of conflict occur within a state, not internationally. Moreover, in many such conflicts, the question of public legitimacy is exactly what is being contested. For example, in the war for independence that resulted in the founding of the United States, just war analysts frequently point out that the rebelling colonies themselves constituted a legitimate public authority and further that the colonies had reasonably concluded that the British government had, in the words of our Declaration of Independence, become "destructive of these ends" of legitimate government and therefore itself had ceased to function as a competent public authority. Indeed, even in cases in which those waging war do not in any plain sense constitute a currently functioning public authority—for example,

the Warsaw ghetto uprising of Polish Jews in 1943 against the Nazi occupation—the legitimate authority requirement of just war theory does not morally invalidate the resort to arms by those resisting oppression by seeking to overthrow illegitimate authority.

26. For example, just war principles often insist that legitimate warfare must be motivated by the intention of enhancing the likelihood of peace and reducing the likelihood of violence and destruction; that it must be proportionate, such that the social goods that would result from victory in war discernibly outweigh the evils that will attend the war; that it must contain the probability of success, such that lives are not taken and sacrificed in futile causes; and that it must pass the test of comparative justice, such that the human goods being defended are important enough and gravely enough in danger to outweigh what many just war theorists view as the standing moral presumption against war. This letter focuses largely on principles of justice in declaring war (in the terminology employed by many Christian just war thinkers, *jus ad bellum*) and in waging war (*jus in bello*). Other principles focus on justice in settling the war and restoring conditions of peace (*jus post bellum*). See Elshtain, ed., *Just War Theory;* U.S. Conference of Catholic Bishops, *The Challenge of Peace: God's Promise and Our Response* (Washington, D.C.: United States Catholic Conference, 1983); and other sources cited in these notes.

27. As of August 19, 2002, official estimates were that 3,043 persons had been killed by the September 11 attackers, including 2,819 in New York, 184 in Washington, and 40 in Pennsylvania. Although this letter refers to "our citizens," included among those murdered on September 11 were many citizens of other countries who were living in the United States at the time of the attack. "Dead and Missing," *New York Times,* April 23, 2002, A13; Thomas J. Lueck, "City Compiles List of Dead and Missing from Sept. 11," *New York Times,* August 20, 2002, B1.

28. In addition to the murders of September 11, members of radical Islamicist organizations are apparently responsible for: the April 18, 1983, bombing of the U.S. Embassy in Beirut, killing 63 persons and injuring 120; the October 23, 1983, bombings of U.S. Marine and French paratroop barracks in Beirut, killing 300 persons; the December 21, 1988, bombing of U.S. Pan Am Flight 103, killing 259 persons; the February 26, 1993, bombing of the World Trade Center in New York City, killing six persons and injuring 1,000; the June 25, 1996, bombing outside the Khobar Towers U.S. military barracks in Dhahran, Saudi Arabia, killing 19 U.S. soldiers and wounding 515; the August 7, 1998, bombing of U.S. embassies in Nairobi, Kenya, and Dar es Salaam, Tanzania, killing 224 persons and injuring more than 5,000; and the October 12, 2000, bombing of the USS *Cole* in Aden, Yemen, killing 17 U.S. sailors and wounding 39. This list is

incomplete (see *Significant Terrorist Incidents, 1961–2001* (Washington, D.C.: U.S. Department of State, Bureau of Public Affairs, October 31, 2001). In addition, members of organizations comprising this movement are also responsible for numerous failed attempts at mass murder, both in the United States and in other countries, including the attempt to bomb the United Nations and the Lincoln and Holland Tunnels in New York in 1993 and the attempt to bomb Los Angeles International Airport on New Year's Eve 2000.

29. The relationship between the jihad and just war traditions is complex. Premodern jihad and just war perspectives overlapped in important ways. Both could legitimate wars aimed at advancing religion, and both sought clearly to disassociate such wars from wars involving indiscriminate or disproportionate tactics. In the modern era, jihad has largely retained its confessional component—that is, its aim of protecting and propagating Islam as a religion. The confessional dimension of jihad thinking in turn seems to be closely linked to the view of the state widely held by Muslim authorities—a view that envisions little or no separation of religion from the state. By contrast, modern Christian thinking on just war has tended to downplay its confessional elements (few Christian theologians today emphasize the value of "crusade"), replacing them with more religiously neutral arguments about human rights and shared moral norms or what some Christian and other thinkers term "natural moral law." Some Muslim scholars today seek, in the case of jihad, more fully to recover the sense of the term as "exertion" or "striving for good" in the service of God, thereby similarly downplaying its confessional elements and emphasizing, for our increasingly plural and interdependent world, the term's more universal dimensions and applications. For example, see Sohail M. Hashmi, "Interpreting the Islamic Ethics of War and Peace," in Nardin, ed., *The Ethics of War and Peace,* 146–66, and Hilmi Zawati, *Is Jihad a Just War? War, Peace, and Human Rights under Islamic and Public International Law* (Lewiston, N.Y.: Edwin Mellen, 2001).

30. For example, Muslim scholars affiliated with the Muslim World League, meeting in Mecca, recently reaffirmed that jihad strictly prohibits "the killing of noncombatants" and attacks against "installations, sites and buildings not related to the fighting." See "Muslim Scholars Define 'Terrorism' as Opposed to Legitimate Jihad," *Middle East News Online,* at www.middleeastwire.com (accessed January 14, 2002). See also Bassam Tibi, "War and Peace in Islam," in Nardin, ed., *The Ethics of War and Peace,* 128–45.

31. The historian Eric Hobsbawm, in his 1995 study of the twentieth century, warns us in particular, as we confront the new millennium, of the emerging crisis of "non-state terrorism," made possible by the growing "privatization of the means of destruction," such that organized groups, operating at least to

some degree independently of public authorities, are increasingly willing and able to perpetrate "violence and wreckage *anywhere* on the globe." Eric Hobsbawm, *Age of Extremes: The Short Twentieth Century 1914–1991* (London: Abacus, 1995), 560.

32. From Abraham Lincoln, "First Inaugural Address," *Abraham Lincoln: Speeches and Writings 1859–1865,* ed. Don E. Fehrenbacher (New York: Library of America, 1989), 223.

# 15

# THIS IS NOT OUR WAR: A LETTER FROM UNITED STATES CITIZENS TO FRIENDS IN EUROPE

*In response to various suggestions, this letter was drafted by Diana Johnstone, a journalist living in Paris; Richard Du Boff, a professor emeritus of economics at Bryn Mawr College; and Edward S. Herman, a professor emeritus of finance at the University of Pennsylvania's Wharton School, who also circulated it requesting signatures. The entire project was carried out over e-mail within a few days at the end of March and the beginning of April 2002. The letter was first published by the French newspaper* Le Monde, *dated April 9, 2002.*

Following the September 11, 2001, suicide attacks on the World Trade Center in New York and the Pentagon in Washington, U.S. President George W. Bush has declared an open-ended "war on terrorism." This war has no apparent limits in place, time, or the extent of destruction that may be inflicted. There is no telling which country may be suspected of hiding "terrorists" or declared to be part of an "axis of evil." The eradication of "evil" could last much longer than the world can withstand the destructive force to be employed. The Pentagon is already launching bombs described as producing the effect of earthquakes and is officially considering the use of nuclear weapons, among other horrors in its constantly improving arsenal. The material destruction envisaged is immeasurable. So is the human damage, not only in terms of lives, but also in terms of the moral desperation and hatred that are certain to be felt by millions of people who can only watch helplessly as their world is devastated by a country, the United States, which assumes that its moral authority is as absolute and unchallengeable as its military power.

We, as United States citizens, have a special responsibility to oppose this mad rush to war. You, as Europeans, also have a special responsibility. Most of your countries are military allies of the United States within NATO. The United States claims to act in self-defense, but also to defend "the interests of its allies and friends." Your countries will inevitably be implicated in U.S. military adventures. Your future is also in jeopardy.

Many informed people both within and outside your governments are aware of the dangerous folly of the war path followed by the Bush administration. But few dare speak out honestly. They are intimidated by the various forms of retaliation that can be taken against "friends" and "allies" who fail to provide unquestioning support. They are afraid of being labeled "anti-American"—the same label absurdly applied to Americans themselves who speak out against war policies and whose protests are easily drowned out in the chorus of chauvinism dominating the U.S. media. A sane and frank European criticism of the Bush administration's war policy can help anti-war Americans make their voices heard.

Celebrating power may be the world's oldest profession among poets and men of letters. As supreme world power, the United States naturally attracts its celebrants who urge the nation's political leaders to go ever farther in using their military might to impose virtue on a recalcitrant world. The theme is age-old and forever the same: The goodness of the powerful should be extended to the powerless by the use of force.

The central fallacy of the pro-war celebrants is the equation between "American values" as understood at home and the exercise of United States economic and especially military power abroad.

Self-celebration is a notorious feature of United States culture, perhaps as a useful means of assimilation in an immigrant society. Unfortunately, September 11 has driven this tendency to new extremes. Its effect is to reinforce a widespread illusion among U.S. citizens that the whole world is fixated, in admiration or in envy, on the United States as it sees itself: prosperous, democratic, generous, welcoming, open to all races and religions, the epitome of universal human values and the last best hope of mankind.

In this ideological context, the question raised after September 11, "Why do they hate us?" has only one answer: "Because we are so good!" Or, as is commonly claimed, they hate us because of "our values."

Most U.S. citizens are unaware that the effect of U.S. power abroad has nothing to do with the "values" celebrated at home, and indeed often serves to deprive people in other countries of the opportunity to attempt to enjoy them should they care to do so.

In Latin America, Africa, and Asia, U.S. power has more often than not been used to prop up the remnants of colonial regimes and unpopular dictators, to impose devastating commercial and financial conditions, to support repressive armed forces, to overthrow or cripple by sanctions relatively independent governments, and finally to send bombers and cruise missiles to rain down death and destruction.

## THE "RIGHT OF SELF-DEFENSE"

### (1) Whose Right?

Since September 11, the United States feels under attack. As a result its government claims a "right to self-defense" enabling it to wage war on its own terms, as it chooses, against any country it designates as an enemy, without proof of guilt or legal procedure.

Obviously, such a "right of self-defense" never existed for countries such as Vietnam, Laos, Cambodia, Libya, Sudan, or Yugoslavia when they were bombed by the United States. Nor will it be recognized for countries bombed by the United States in the future. This is simply the right of the strongest, the law of the jungle. Exercising such a "right," denied all others, cannot serve "universal values" but only undermines the very concept of a world order based on universal values with legal recourse open to all on a basis of equality.

A "right" enjoyed only by one entity—the most powerful—is not a right but a privilege exercised only to the detriment of the rights of others.

### (2) How Is the United States to "Defend" Itself?

Supposedly in self-defense, the United States launched a war against Afghanistan. This was not an action specially designed to respond to the

unique events of September 11. On the contrary, it was exactly what the
United States was already doing, and had already planned to do, as outlined in Pentagon documents: bomb other countries, send military
forces onto foreign soil, and topple their governments. The United
States is openly planning an all-out war—not excluding use of nuclear
weapons—against Iraq, a country it has been bombing for a decade,
with the proclaimed aim of replacing its government with leaders selected by Washington.

## (3) Precisely What Is Being "Defended?"

What is being defended is related to what was attacked.

Traditionally, "defense" means defense of national territory. On September 11, an attack actually took place on and against U.S. territory.
This was not a conventional attack by a major power designed to seize
territory. Rather, it was an anonymous strike against particular targeted
institutions. In the absence of any claim of responsibility, the symbolic
nature of the targets may have been assumed to be self-explanatory. The
World Trade Center clearly symbolized U.S. global economic power,
while the Pentagon represented U.S. military power. Thus, it seems
highly unlikely that the September 11 attacks were symbolically directed against "American values" as celebrated in the United States.

Rather, the true target seems to have been U.S. economic and military power as it is projected abroad. According to reports, fifteen of the
nineteen identified hijackers were Saudi Arabians hostile to the presence of U.S. military bases on Saudi soil. September 11 suggests that the
nation projecting its power abroad is vulnerable at home, but the real issue is U.S. intervention abroad. Indeed the Bush wars are designed precisely to defend and strengthen U.S. power abroad. It is U.S. global
power projection that is being defended, not domestic freedoms and
way of life.

In reality, foreign wars are more likely to undermine the domestic
values cherished by civilians at home than to defend or spread them.
But governments that wage aggressive wars always drum up domestic
support by convincing ordinary people that war is necessary to defend
or to spread noble ideas. The principal difference between the imperial
wars of the past and the global thrust of the United States today is the

far greater means of destruction available. The disproportion between the material power of destruction and the constructive power of human wisdom has never been more dangerously unbalanced. Intellectuals today have the choice of joining the chorus of those who celebrate brute force by rhetorically attaching it to "spiritual values," or taking up the more difficult and essential task of exposing the arrogant folly of power and working with the whole of humanity to create means of reasonable dialogue, fair economic relations, and equal justice.

The right to self-defense must be a collective human right. Humanity as a whole has the right to defend its own survival against the "self-defense" of an unchecked superpower. For half a century, the United States has repeatedly demonstrated its indifference to the collateral death and destruction wrought by its self-proclaimed efforts to improve the world. Only by joining in solidarity with the victims of U.S. military power can we in the rich countries defend whatever universal values we claim to cherish.

## SIGNATORIES (AS OF APRIL 10, 2002)

Daphne Abeel, *journalist, Cambridge, Massachusetts;* Julie L. Abraham, *professor of English, New York City;* Michael Albert, *ZNet, Boston;* Janet Kestenberg Amighi, *anthropologist, Hahneman University, Philadelphia;* Electa Arenal, *Hispanic and Luso-Brazilian literatures, City University of New York;* Anthony Arnove, *editor/publisher, South End Press, Boston;* Stanley Aronowitz, *Center for Cultural Studies, City University of New York;* Dean Baker, *economist, Center for Economic and Policy Research, Washington, D.C.;* Houston A. Baker Jr., *Duke University;* David Barsamian, *director, Alternative Radio, Boulder, Colorado;* Rosalyn Baxandall, *chair of American studies, State University of New York at Old Westbury;* Medea Benjamin, *founding director, Global Exchange, San Francisco;* Dick Bennett, *professor emeritus, University of Arkansas;* Larry Bensky, *KPFA/Pacifica Radio;* Norman Birnbaum, *professor emeritus, Georgetown University Law Center;* Joel Bleifuss, *editor, In These Times, Chicago;* Chana Bloch, *professor of English, Mills College;* William Blum, *author, Washington, D.C.;* Magda Bogin, *writer, Columbia University;* Patrick Bond, *University of the Witwatersrand;* Charles P. Boyer, *professor of mathematics, University of New Mexico;* Francis A. Boyle, *professor of international law, University of Illinois;* Gray Brechin, *Department of Geography, University of*

*California, Berkeley;* Renate Bridenthal, *professor emerita of history, City University of New York;* Linda Bullard, *environmentalist, USA/Europe;* Judith Butler, *University of California, Berkeley;* Bob Buzzanco, *professor of history, University of Houston;* Helen Caldicott, *pediatrician, author, and founder of Physicians for Social Responsibility;* John Cammett, *historian, New York;* Stephanie M. H. Camp, *assistant professor of history, University of Washington;* Ward Churchill, *author, Boulder, Colorado;* John P. Clark, *professor of philosophy, Loyola University, New Orleans;* Dan Coughlin, *radio executive director, Washington, D.C.;* Sandi Cooper, *historian, New York;* Lawrence Davidson, *professor of Middle East history, West Chester University;* David Devine, *professor of English, Paris;* Douglas Dowd, *economist, Bologna, San Francisco;* Madhu Dubey, *professor of English and Africana studies, Brown University;* Richard B. Du Boff, *Bryn Mawr College;* Peter Erlinder, *past president, National Lawyers Guild, and law professor, St. Paul, Minnesota;* Francis Feeley, *professor of American studies, Université Stendhal, Grenoble;* Richard Flynn, *professor of literature and philosophy, Georgia Southern University;* Michael S. Foley, *assistant professor of history, City University of New York;* John Bellamy Foster, *Eugene, Oregon;* H. Bruce Franklin, *professor of English and American studies, Rutgers University;* Jane Franklin, *author and historian, Montclair, New Jersey;* Oscar H. Gandy Jr., *Annenberg School for Communication, University of Pennsylvania;* Jamshed Ghandhi, *Wharton School, University of Pennsylvania;* Larry Gross, *Annenberg School for Communication, University of Pennsylvania;* Beau Grosscup, *professor of International Relations, California State University, Chico;* Zalmay Gulzad, *professor of Asian-American studies, Loyola University, Chicago;* Thomas J. Gumbleton, *auxiliary bishop, Roman Catholic Archdiocese of Detroit;* Marilyn Hacker, *professor of English, City College of New York;* Robin Hahnel, *professor of economics, American University, Washington, D.C.;* Edward S. Herman, *economist and media analyst, Philadelphia;* Marc W. Herold, *University of New Hampshire;* John L. Hess, *journalist and correspondent, New York City;* David U. Himmelstein, M.D., *associate professor of medicine, Harvard Medical School;* W. G. Huff, *University of Glasgow;* Adrian Prentice Hull, *California State University, Monterey Bay;* Marsha Hurst, *director, Health Advocacy Program, Sarah Lawrence College, New York;* David Isles, *associate professor of mathematics, Tufts University;* Robert Jensen, *School of Journalism, University of Texas;* Diana Johnstone, *journalist, Paris;* John Jonik, *political cartoonist/activist, Philadelphia;* Louis Kampf, *professor emeritus of literature, Massachusetts Institute of Technology;* Mary Kaye, *professor of fine arts, Art Institute of Boston, Lesley University;* Douglas Kellner, *University of California, Los Angeles;* Michael King, *senior news editor, Austin Chronicle, Austin, Texas;* Gabriel Kolko, *author, Amsterdam;* Joyce

Kolko, *author, Amsterdam;* Claudia Koonz, *professor of history, Duke University;* Joel Kovel, *Bard College;* Marilyn Krysl, writer, *University of Colorado;* Mark Lance, *Program on Philosophy, Justice, and Peace, Georgetown University;* Ann J. Lane, *University of Virginia;* Karen Latuchie, *book editor, New Jersey;* Peggy Law, *executive director, International Media Project, Oakland, California;* Amy Schrager Lang, *associate professor of American studies, Cambridge, Massachusetts;* Helena Lewis, *historian, Harvard University Humanities Center;* Dave Lindorff, *journalist, Maple Glen, Pennsylvania;* Eric Lott, *professor of English, University of Virginia;* Angus Love, *Esq., Narberth, Pennsylvania;* David MacMichael, *director, Association of National Security Alumni, Washington, D.C.;* Harry Magdoff, *coeditor, Monthly Review, New York City;* Sanjoy Mahajan, *physicist, University of Cambridge;* Michael Marcus, *Department of Mathematics, City College of New York;* Robert McChesney, *University of Illinois;* Jo Ann McNamara, *historian emerita, Hunter College, New York;* Arthur Mitzman, *emeritus professor of modern history, University of Amsterdam;* Margaret E. Montoya, *professor, School of Law, University of New Mexico;* Robert Naiman, *Center for Economic and Policy Research, Washington, D.C.;* Marilyn Nelson, *poet/professor, University of Connecticut;* Suzanne Oboler, *University of Illinois, Chicago;* Bertell Ollman, *Department of Politics, New York University;* Alicia Ostriker, *professor of English, Rutgers University;* Christian Parenti, *author, New College of California;* Michael Parenti, *author, Berkeley, California;* Mark Pavlick, *Georgetown University, Washington, D.C.;* Michael Perelman, *professor of economics, California State University, Chico;* Jeff Perlstein, *executive director, Media Alliance, San Francisco;* David Peterson, *writer and researcher, Chicago;* James Petras, *State University of New York at Binghamton;* Joan Pinkham, *translator, Amherst, Massachusetts;* Lawrence Pinkham, *professor emeritus of journalism, University of Massachusetts;* Cathie Platt, *licensed professional counselor, Charlottesville, Virginia;* Gordon Poole, *Istituto Universitario Orientale, Naples, Italy;* Douglas Porpora, *professor of sociology, Drexel University, Philadelphia;* Larry Portis, *American Studies, Université Paul Valéry, Montpellier, France;* Ellen Ray, *Institute for Media Analysis, New York City;* Elton Rayack, *professor of economics emeritus, University of Rhode Island;* Lillian S. Robinson, *Simone de Beauvoir Institute, Concordia University, Montreal;* Rick Rozoff, *medical social worker, Chicago;* Sten Rudstrom, *theater artist, Berlin;* William H. Schaap, *Institute for Media Analysis, New York City;* Ellen Schrecker, *Yeshiva University, New York City;* Gretchen Seifert, *artist and photographer, Chicago;* Anne Shaver, *professor emerita of English, Denison University;* Gerald E. Shenk, *Social and Behavioral Sciences Center, California State University, Seaside;* Mary Shepard, *media critic, St. Paul, Minnesota;* Francis Shor, *professor, Wayne State University;* Robert M.

Smith, *Brandywine Peace Community, Swarthmore, Pennsylvania;* Alan Sokal, *professor of physics, New York University;* Norman Solomon, *author and syndicated columnist, San Francisco;* William S. Solomon, *Rutgers University;* Sarah Standefer, *nurse, Minneapolis;* Abraham Sussman, *clinical psychologist, Cambridge, Massachusetts;* Malcolm Sylvers, *University of Venice;* Paul M. Sweezy, *coeditor, Monthly Review, New York City;* Holly Thau, *psychotherapist, Oregon;* Reetika Vazirani, *writer, New Jersey;* Gore Vidal, *writer, Los Angeles;* Joe Volk, *Friends Committee on National Legislation, Washington, D.C.;* Lynne Walker, *historian, London;* Karin Wilkins, *University of Texas at Austin;* Howard Winant, *Temple University;* Steffie Woolhandler, M.D., M.P.H., *associate professor of medicine, Harvard Medical School;* George Wright, *Department of Political Science, California State University, Chico;* Howard Zinn, *writer, Boston.*

# National Service

**16**

# PUTTING PATRIOTISM
# INTO PRACTICE

## Senator John McCain

**S**ince September 11, Americans have found a new spirit of national unity and purpose. Forty years ago, at the height of the Cold War, President John F. Kennedy challenged Americans to enter into public service. Today, confronted with a challenge no less daunting than the Cold War, Americans again are eager for ways to serve at home and abroad. Government should make it easier for them to do so.

What is lacking today is not a need for patriotic service or a willingness to serve but the opportunity. Indeed, one of the curious truths of our era is that while opportunities to serve ourselves have exploded—with ever-expanding choices of what to buy, where to eat, and what to read, watch, or listen to—opportunities to spend some time serving our country have narrowed. The high cost of campaigning keeps many idealistic people from running for public office. Teacher-certification requirements keep talented people out of the classroom. The all-volunteer military is looking for lifers, not those who might want to serve for shorter tours of duty.

## THE AMERICORPS EXCEPTION

The one big exception to this trend is AmeriCorps, the program of national service started by President Bill Clinton. Since 1994, nearly

250,000 Americans have served one- to two-year stints in AmeriCorps, tutoring school children, building low-income housing, or helping flood-ravaged communities. AmeriCorps members receive a small stipend and $4,725 in college aid for their service. But the real draw is the chance to have an adventure and accomplish something important. And AmeriCorps' achievements are indeed impressive: thousands of homes constructed, hundreds of thousands of senior citizens assisted to live independently in their own homes, and millions of children taught, tutored, or mentored.

Beyond accomplishing these good deeds, AmeriCorps has transformed the lives of young people who have participated in its ranks. They have begun to glimpse the glory of serving the cause of freedom. They have come to know the obligations and rewards of active citizenship.

Though some early critics of the program, myself included, feared that AmeriCorps members would elbow out other volunteers, they have done the opposite. AmeriCorps members are typically put to work recruiting, training, and supervising volunteers. For instance, most of the more than 500 AmeriCorps members who work for Habitat for Humanity spend less time swinging hammers themselves than making sure that hammers, nails, and drywall are at the work site when the volunteers arrive. They then teach the volunteers the basic skills of how to hang drywall. As a result, studies show that each AmeriCorps member generates, on average, nine additional volunteers.

But for all its concrete achievements, AmeriCorps has a fundamental flaw: In its seven years of existence, it has barely stirred the nation's imagination. In 1961, President Kennedy launched the Peace Corps to make good on his famous challenge, "Ask not what your country can do for you, but rather what you can do for your country." Since then, more than 162,000 Americans have served in the Peace Corps, and the vast majority of Americans today have heard of the organization. By contrast, more than 200,000 Americans have served in AmeriCorps, yet two out of three Americans say they have never heard of the program.

In addition, AmeriCorps members often take on the identity of the organizations they're assigned to. In the process, they often lose any sense of being part of a larger national service enterprise, if they ever had it at all. Indeed, staffers at nonprofit groups sometimes call Ameri-Corps headquarters looking for support for their organizations, only to find out that *their own salaries* are being paid by AmeriCorps. It's no wonder most Americans say they have never heard of the program. And a program few have heard of will obviously not be able to inspire a new ethic of national service.

## THE NEXT STEP

If we are to have a resurgence of patriotic service in this country, then programs such as AmeriCorps must be expanded and changed in ways that inspire the nation. There should be more focus on meeting national goals and on making short-term service, both civilian and military, a rite of passage for young Americans.

That is why Senator Evan Bayh and I introduced legislation to revamp national service programs and dramatically expand opportunities for public service. Many tasks lie ahead, both new and old. On the home front, there are new security and civil defense requirements, such as increased police and border patrol needs. We will charge the Corporation for National Service, the federal office that oversees national volunteer programs, with the task of assembling a plan that would put civilians to work to assist the Office of Homeland Security. The military will need new recruits to confront the challenges abroad, so our bill would also improve benefits for our service members.

At the same time, because the society we defend needs increased services, from promoting literacy to caring for the elderly, we will expand AmeriCorps and senior service programs to enlarge our national army of volunteers. Currently, more than 50,000 volunteers serve in Ameri-Corps. Under our bill, 250,000 volunteers each year would be able to answer the call—with half of them assisting in civil defense needs and half continuing the good work of AmeriCorps.

We must also ask our nation's colleges to promote service more aggressively. Currently, many colleges devote only a small fraction of federal work-study funds to community service, while the majority of federal resources are used to fill low-skill positions. This was not Congress' vision when it passed the Higher Education Act of 1965. Under our bill, universities will be required to promote student involvement in community activities more vigorously.

We also seek to better enable seniors fifty-five years and older to serve their communities in a variety of capacities, including education, long-term care, and serving as foster grandparents. Our legislation removes the low-income requirement for participation in all three Senior Service programs, provides low-income seniors with a stipend for service, and creates a competitive grant program to provide seniors with training to both prepare and encourage them to serve.

And for those who might consider serving their country in the armed forces, the benefits must keep pace with the times. While the volunteer military has been successful, our armed forces continue to suffer from significant recruitment challenges.

Our legislation encourages more young Americans to serve in the military by allowing the Department of Defense to create a new, shorter-term enlistment option. This "18-18-18" plan would offer an $18,000 bonus—in addition to regular pay—for eighteen months of active duty and eighteen months of reserve duty. And we would significantly improve education payments made to service members under current law.

Public service is a virtue. This is the right moment to issue a new call to service and give a new generation a way to claim the rewards and responsibilities of active citizenship.

## NOTE

The military component of the McCain-Bayh Call to Service Act was passed by Congress on November 13, 2002 as part of a defense authorization bill. Under the act, individuals who volunteer for a short-term military enlistment track would be required to serve on active duty for fifteen months in the Armed Services, but they could complete the remainder of their military service obligation by choosing service on active or reserve duty. The reserve obligation could be fulfilled by serving in a civilian national service program such as the Peace Corps or AmeriCorps. In return for service, the legislation provides a choice of incentives, including a $5,000 bonus, repayment of a student loan up to $18,000, or an educational allowance under the Montgomery GI Bill. —JHM

## ❿

# A NEW DRAFT FOR A NEW TIME

## Paul Glastris

**P**resident Bill Clinton made the point in speeches after September 11 that terror—the deliberate killing of noncombatants for economic, political, or religious reasons—has a long history; in fact, it's as old as combat itself. And yet it has never succeeded as a military strategy on its own, and it's not going to today. America will survive this. But it is also true that in war, defenses usually lag behind offenses. And that is where America is today. Our ability to defend ourselves against terrorism lags far, far behind the ability of terrorists to inflict damage on us.

So regardless, then, of our successes in Afghanistan, President George W. Bush is right when he says—and he has said it repeatedly—that this is going to be a long, long war, and a war unlike any we have ever fought. In the search for precedents, people have talked about World War II. A number of people have pointed out, though, including my colleague Charlie Moskos, that a better precedent is the Cold War—more like 1948 than 1941. Like then, we are probably at the beginning of what could be a decades-long struggle that will only occasionally be played out on the battlefield but that will nevertheless demand a reordering of our national priorities and a vast amount of treasure and attention.

The only question is, How will we mobilize our nation to fight it? Are we going to rely solely on our professional military and security forces— our Coast Guard, Border Patrol, Federal Emergency Management

Agency, and so forth? Or are we going to supplement that effort by asking average citizens to take a role in their own defense? And if so, will we—can we—rely on volunteers? Or do we do what America has always done in major wars, including the first decades of the Cold War, and require service by instituting a draft?

## DEFENSIVE NEEDS

I believe that we do need a draft and that we needed one long before September 11. The draft is sort of like an army knife: It does a lot of things very, very well. But because this is a new kind of war, we need a new kind of draft—one that would focus less on preparing men for conventional combat than on training young men and even young women for the arguably more daunting task of guarding against and responding to terrorism here at home.

There has been a heartening resurgence of voluntary service in recent years. We all know that, and it's exciting and tempting to think that this new ethos of volunteerism, plus a bit more spending on the military and national security, will solve the problem. But it's my feeling that that's not the case. There's a reason America has instituted a draft in past wars, and that's because volunteers don't fill uniforms. Soon after the events of September 11, for instance, newspapers reported that the phones in military recruitment offices were ringing off the hook. Follow-up stories showed that all the clamor had brought, as far as we can tell, virtually no increase in new recruits. Our patriotism, though sincerely felt, has so far amounted to flag-waving.

The need for more manpower is clear. The U.S. military actions in Afghanistan, though modest by historical standards, necessitated the call-up of large numbers of reservists. Many reservists work as police officers, firefighters, and emergency medical technicians—in other words, we are draining our municipalities of precisely the people we are going to need if and when another terrorist attack happens. In addition to that, we are likely to need thousands more men and women in uniform to guard airports, dams, nuclear power plants, sports complexes, and U.S. embassies. We are going to need more border patrol and customs agents to keep terrorists at bay. We are going to need more Immigration and

Naturalization Service agents to track down immigrants who have over-stayed their visas, Coast Guard personnel to inspect ships, air marshals, and FBI agents to uncover terrorist cells.

## STANDING UP FOR A DRAFT

Where are all these brave men and women going to come from? We are a rich society; we can certainly offer substantial salaries. But the fact is, even in a weak economy, there is a finite number of competent people willing to choose a career that requires wearing a uniform, performing often-dull work, such as guard duty, with alertness, and occasionally be-ing asked to put their lives at risk. Police departments all over the coun-try prior to September 11 were already having a hard time filling their ranks. The armed forces have had to double starting pay to get half as many recruits as they did in 1989, and there are those who argue, and I think it's probably true just from my discussions with recruiters, that the quality of new recruits is not what it should be.

A draft is the best way to meet the needs for both military and home-land security as well as for the national service idea, which has been gaining support wisely, and I think rightly, for the past few years. Previ-ous generations of Americans would not have thought twice about this. The curious thing is the deep psychological resistance many people have to simply talking about a draft. One of the funniest things about being in Washington is that you talk to think-tank people and congressional people who say, "You know personally I think the draft is a great idea, but . . ." And the "but" is, it will never happen. It's almost like meeting a fellow mason—oh, you're a mason too?—there's a whole room full of masons, but no one will actually say it. And I think there just simply isn't an institution or politician anywhere in our capital who can stand up and say, "I favor the draft," even though they personally may favor it.

So I want to state what it is I would like to see in the way of a draft: a three-tiered system, not unlike what they have in places such as Ger-many, where eighteen- to twenty-five-year-olds all would serve. But they would have something that's never really happened in a draft before but that I think is very important in this day and age, and that is to have choice. And the choice would be whether to serve in the military, in a homeland security role, or in what we might call traditional national service—working for Habitat for Humanity, working for AmeriCorps, and so forth. At least the latter two of these, in my opinion, should not just be open to women but should demand participation of them as well. And I think we could probably have a healthy discussion about whether to include women in the military draft.

At the end of these eighteen-month to two-year stints, each volunteer would get a GI Bill type of assistance for college. Both the length of service and the amount of the assistance would be tailored to the danger of the tasks. So if you're doing peacekeeping duty in Kosovo or standing guard at a nuclear power plant, you would probably get a bit more in the end. But the point would be everyone would serve. And as we all know, during the Vietnam War, opting to fulfill one's draft requirement stateside was considered a way to save your skin. Obviously, that's no longer true.

As we've seen with the New York firefighters, it can be dangerous work.

## NOTE

This chapter was originally published in *The Responsive Community* 12, no. 2 (spring 2002): 40–43.

# 18

# CITIZENSHIP AND SACRIFICE

## Michael Lind

National service has always been the bridesmaid but never the bride in American politics. From the time the idea of some kind of service more comprehensive than military duty in the militia or in the conscript army became popular in the early 1900s, it has had a lot of support—mostly on the center–left, some on the right. But national service has never really gotten very far. Now, after a century of failed attempts, we have had proposals for some comprehensive service programs at the federal level.

It behooves us to ask why this idea has failed so often. Universal military training was proposed by General Leonard Wood after World War I, and there were people who wanted to revive the Civilian Conservation Corps after World War II, but they got nowhere. There was a big debate in the 1980s, and that got nowhere, either. I think we ought to look at this and ask, What are the arguments against national service that at least the majority of policymakers and the public found compelling then? Are they still valid—or at least are they going to persuade a majority of people, whether they're valid or not?

My colleague Ted Halstead has mentioned three different rationales for national service, and I think this is a useful and constructive way of thinking about it. Two of these rationales, when it comes to the subject of a draft, are extraordinarily weak. They may be good arguments for some voluntary form of service, but not if conscription or coercion is involved. Only one argument in favor of national service is very powerful. The three that he has mentioned are the unmet-needs argument, which holds that there are not enough people helping out in nursing homes, there's too much litter along the highway, there's a need to build park benches in the national parks, and so on; the character-building argument, or that people should not go for their entire education without encountering someone from a different race, a different socioeconomic background, or a different religion; and a final argument based on practical military needs and homeland defense.

It seems to me to be a mistake for proponents of national service to say prematurely that we'll have the biggest possible coalition of supporters while we agree to disagree about what the purpose of national service is. I think this has hurt many of the efforts in the past. There has to be a hierarchy among these purposes, and, as I say, two of them are very weak, and one of them is very strong.

## UNMET NEEDS

The weakest, in my opinion, is the unmet-needs argument. In most cases this takes the form of an assertion rather than an argument. It's very subjective to say that there are needs that are not being met, not only by the private sector marketplace but also by our very flourishing, philanthropic, nonprofit, foundation-based, church-based, civil society. Depending on whom you ask, we have an unmet need in bringing the arts to poor children if you're on the relative left. If you're on the relative right, you might say there's an unmet need in providing manpower to faith-based church institutions.

Assuming that you can get a majority of Americans to agree on a list of unmet needs, it seems to me that you then have to go through a second process: You have to ask, Can the marketplace take care of this? And if the market can't do it, then can nonprofit organizations or churches or other institutions in our existing noncoercive, nonconscriptive civil society do this? When you're dealing with the power of the state, with something like the draft, it's not enough to say that there are not enough people helping the elderly in nursing homes because of the prices of elder care. You first have to establish that you can't pay more money for adult professionals with benefits and perhaps union representation to do these jobs. And even if you can establish that, you have to say why this job must be done by the government. Why the federal government? Why not instead by the nonprofit sector, which could have a greater foreseeable role? We tend to forget about this and think it's just a question of the market or the state, but we have the world's most developed nonprofit sector.

So I think that the unmet-needs argument is the least convincing argument for a draft. In a country with our own individualistic, libertarian traditions, you cannot, in essence, enslave eighteen-year-olds to do things that might be inspiring for a nonprofit organization to do, such as beautifying highways and helping the elderly. I use the term "enslavement" just to be provocative, as a supporter of the military draft. When you're talking about forced labor, the alternative to which is imprisonment, you have to have very good reasons for it. And having better highways and more beautiful national parks and emptying bedpans is just not a compelling enough reason for involuntary servitude to the government.

## CHARACTER BUILDING

I don't think that character building and class mixing, as much as I support both of those, are compelling reasons for a draft, either. We've now had a generation of Americans since the Vietnam War, maybe a couple of generations of affluent kids, who have essentially lived in a socioeconomic bubble. They have managed to go from birth through school through prep school through the Ivy League without encountering anyone from outside their rarefied social stratum. I think it would be good for the souls of these kids if they went out and helped the poor or helped teach children remedial instruction or even went and dug ditches. It might be good for their souls, but I don't think they should be drafted. Frankly, I don't think the federal government is in the character-building business.

The use of government coercion to shape the character of citizens goes against the American tradition—both American traditions, really. The deepest American traditions are the Jeffersonian and the Hamiltonian traditions. Both of these are uneasy with the national service tradition, which comes out of English Fabianism and certain aspects of the social-ist tradition. The Jeffersonians love the idea of the citizen soldier, but only at the local level. The whole point of the local militia was to restrain federal government, so you can't simply transfer the Jeffersonian model to the national government. The militia is intended as a check on Wash-ington, and national service, even for the military, inspires uneasiness among right-wing militia types who are genuine, although somewhat neurotic, Jeffersonians. To make matters worse, from a Jeffersonian per-spective, drafting people to perform civilian functions is just slavery, so no Jeffersonian could support that.

The other tradition in the United States is the Hamiltonian tradition, which supports a strong centralized government, a powerful military, and a powerful central intelligence agency. At the same time, however, the Hamiltonians love the division of labor, they love capitalism, they love commerce, and they also love expertise. Everything Alexander Hamilton says about the militia in the Federalist Papers is an insult. He was the number-one aide to Washington during the Revolutionary War, and both Washington and Hamilton were terribly frustrated with the performance of the militia. This was the experience of many subsequent leaders, including one of our greatest generals, General Winfield Scott, in the Mexican–American War. Scott got so disgusted with the militia's incompetence that he sent them all home in the middle of the war. And he won the war with only his handpicked regular troops. It was with a great sense of relief in the twentieth century that most military leaders turned to creating a professional full-time military instead of relying on what was, in some cases, little more than a local rural rabble with mus-kets, which often ran amok and was very difficult to control. So there's a real tension between American tradition and the idea that the federal government can simply conscript you for a period of time to perform functions that are not absolutely and immediately justified by necessity.

## MILITARY NEEDS

It's the third argument, the military argument, that Americans have found compelling. If there is no way to defend the country adequately with your professional military (and that includes having the level of expertise and the educational credentials you want in your soldiers), there seems to me to be a compelling practical argument for a draft in order to meet manpower needs alone.

In addition, there is a moral argument that is more subjective. It is the idea that in a republic, as opposed to the old-fashioned despotic monarchies, the citizens participate, they are the owners of the state, the state does not own them. The republican ideal is not socialism but rather something like a property owners' association: in return for being associated, you take part in the administration of justice through being a juror, you take part in the selection of leaders through voting (which used to be considered a duty, not a hobby), and you take part in defense, at least locally, through the militia. This republican ideal has faded away, and in practice our relationship with the government is largely one of paying taxes. If you never have jury duty and you don't vote and you never serve in the military, there is very little difference between living in twenty-first-century America and being an eighteenth-century Hessian subject of King George.

So there is both a moral and a practical argument for military conscription. And as Paul Glastris has suggested, September 11 possibly has transformed this debate about the military aspect of national service. For the first time since the early or middle twentieth century, homeland defense is something that is very important, very significant. Homeland defense is not an afterthought, it's not a way of avoiding the draft. Homeland defense is actually something serious.

This leads me to draw conclusions that may hearten some and dishearten others. I think that a two-tiered program of national service, which gives you the choice between military service abroad and homeland defense within the borders of the United States, can be justified. Conscription for the purpose of homeland defense seems plausible— that is, it doesn't look as though you're simply in favor of national service on principle and you've come up with an excuse for it. No, it's something we really need to do.

What would these homeland defenders do? Well, they could provide emergency personnel support for EMS units, firefighters, and police. You would want professionals to be on the front lines, but in a lot of cases people would be needed to drive ambulances, answer phones, arrange those logistics behind the scenes.

Frankly, I don't consider the admirable activities such as many of those associated with AmeriCorps or VISTA as a legitimate alternative to homeland defense or to serving in the military. It seems to me you are at least in theory risking your life if you are responding to a tornado, helping firefighters respond to a terrorist bombing, or helping hospitals during bioterrorism attacks. There is the same connection between personal and physical labor and sacrifice and citizenship that war abroad has historically had. Now with all due respect to the proponents of other kinds of civilian national service, I don't think that helping young children learn to read, picking up litter on the highways, or helping the elderly in understaffed nursing homes is comparable.

The contemporary debate on national service was started by William James in his essay "The Moral Equivalent of War."[1] I will conclude by saying that I don't think that most civilian service is the moral equivalent of war. The connection between citizenship and sacrifice lies in actually putting yourself in harm's way. I think that the argument of national defense is the most compelling argument for national service, especially if it uses the draft. And I suspect that for most of the public, it's the only compelling argument.

## NOTES

This chapter was originally published in *The Responsive Community* 12, no. 2 (spring 2002): 44–49.

1. William James, *The Moral Equivalent of War, and Other Essays: And Selections from Some Problems of Philosophy* (New York: Harper & Row, 1971).

# III

# AMERICAN SOCIETY
# AFTER SEPTEMBER 11

**（19）**

# A STRONGER NATION

## Alan Wolfe

The terrorist attacks against the United States, meant to divide Americans from one another, have united them as at no time since World War II. Immediately before the events, we were still discussing the 2000 presidential election and whether the person elected with more blue states than red ones—or was it the other way around?—held office legitimately. The issues we debated then included whether frozen embryos were human beings and whether the Boy Scouts could exclude homosexuals from their ranks. People talked seriously about a deep chasm between one America that was presumed to be devout and another that was routinely described as secular. Political speculation focused on whether President George W. Bush could cut taxes and expand the military at the same time and what the Democrats would do to ensure that he could not. And underlying the whole discussion, a debate was taking place over whether Americans were losing their sense of civic participation and concern for the direction of their society.

It takes a real war to make Americans realize how insignificant our culture war has been. Twice in recent years, Americans have been victims of murderous terrorist attacks at home: one took place in Oklahoma, the other in lower Manhattan and on the outskirts of Washington, D.C. Oklahoma, in many ways the most conservative state in the union, symbolizes the side in the culture war that stands for a return to the religion, values, and morality of years past. Lower Manhattan, probably the most liberal slice of America, represents modern urbane cosmopolitanism, racial and ethnic diversity, and openness to the rest of the world. And Washington, as the nation's capital, stands in the conservative mind for big government and in the liberal mind as the embodiment of U.S. military power. Yet what the terrorists proved by their acts is that, no matter how different Americans may be from one another in their religious beliefs or political views, they are all equal before the onslaught of machinery transformed into weapons. The United States really is one nation, even if it needs other nations, or international bandits without a nation, to remind it of that fact.

America was the target of the September 11 attacks because its commitments to free speech, religious liberty, gender equality, and racial and ethnic diversity were intolerable to theocrats persuaded that only one truth exists and that it is their mission to ensure that no one thinks otherwise. The United States was made vulnerable to terrorist attack because it has open borders, a dedication to civil liberties, an aversion to discrimination on the basis of group characteristics, a free market, and a strong belief that the pursuit of the good life and the quest for zealotry are incompatible. How much will change as a result of September 11? Certainly airport security will be tightened, electronic and other forms of communication will be more closely monitored, and police will be more forthright in their use of profiling—racial and otherwise—to stop violent acts before they happen. But none of these steps will change America's commitment to liberal and democratic values. Instead, the most likely effect of the terrorist attacks will be to strengthen American liberties by grounding them in reality and underscoring why we value them in the first place.

## RELIGIOUS DIFFERENCE

Illustrative of what is likely to emerge in the America shaped by the events of September 11 is a firmer sense of the proper role for religion in a society no longer shaped by a common faith tradition. Although the Constitution formally separated church and state, America was nonetheless governed throughout the nineteenth century by an unofficial Protestant morality that structured its educational system, political values, approach to child rearing, work ethic, and even foreign policy. As Catholics and Jews increasingly made the United States their home, however, the nation's understanding of morality could no longer be based on the assumptions of one faith. Not without serious conflict, American morality did change. For a time, the term "Christian" came to replace "Protestant" in descriptions of the nation so as to include Catholics. Then, as the country fought a war against the most anti-Semitic regime in modern history, it broadened the description once again to "Judeo-Christian," even though Jews and Christians had been fighting each other for 2,000 years.

Before September 11, there were already more Muslims in the United States than Episcopalians—and it is only a matter of time before adherents of Islam replace Jews as the largest non-Christian religious group in the country. Scholars were engaged in an effort to develop a replacement term for "Judeo-Christian" that would cover this new reality, with "Abrahamic" emerging as the leading candidate, since Muslims, like Jews and Christians, trace their origins back to Abraham. Although this term has its limits—it does not encompass Hinduism, Buddhism, or many other religions now practiced by large numbers of Americans—it does continue a long-standing process of recognizing the increasing religious diversity that characterizes American society. When President Bush spoke at a Washington mosque on September 17, praising Muslims for their "incredibly valuable contribution to our country," his words could be understood as an official recognition of post-Judeo-Christian America. (And when, in the aftermath of attacks on turban-wearing Sikhs across the country he invited a group of Sikhs to the White House to reassure them, he moved beyond "Abrahamic" religions as well.) It took an act of Middle Eastern terrorists to make Americans realize that many peaceful, hardworking, and law-abiding Muslims live in their country.

Just as Americans have learned something about their religious diversity from the attacks launched on them, they have also learned something about the proper role for religion in a society committed to separation of church and state. Before September 11, the U.S. Supreme Court tended to draw a sharp wall between these two institutions. In

June 2000, for example, the Court ruled that prayers before a high school football game, amplified over loudspeakers, created a coercive atmosphere and thus amounted to an unconstitutional establishment of religion. Although the Court's jurisprudence in this area has often been inconsistent (it has also ruled that student fees collected at a public university cannot be denied to a conservative Christian student publication), the trend of at least some of its decisions has been in the direction of questioning an active role for faith in the American public square.

Yet in response to the terrorist attacks, the country's entire political elite assembled in the National Cathedral and was led in prayer by religious leaders of many faiths—and no one thought to object. The fact that religion and politics were so seamlessly blended and that no danger to the republic followed from their mixture suggests that in an emergency the right balance will be found. One side in the debate over religion and politics can take heart from the fact that Americans, even when they assemble in public, need the healing that faith offers to overcome tragedy. And the other side can recognize that, under contemporary conditions of religious diversity, no single religious point of view will be used to coerce others. The World Trade Center and Pentagon attacks brought out common sense on one of our most contentious issues, a lesson that may be found useful as future Court decisions are handed down in this area.

One American who showed no appreciation for common sense in the days following the attacks was the Reverend Jerry Falwell, and one of the more important cultural responses since September 11 has been the widespread revulsion against his hateful message blaming gays, feminists, and civil libertarians for the tragedy. In an odd way, the terrorists were more egalitarian than Falwell: They cared not a whit whether the Americans they killed were gay or straight, left wing or right wing, devout or secular, male or female, black or white—or even whether they were Americans. Hatred that indiscriminate reminds us why more discriminate forms of hatred are un-American. As long as Falwell was viewed as a man who might deliver votes, politicians bent over backward to appease him. Now that he is rightly seen as a man who instead delivers hate, they will avoid him. Falwell's intolerance establishes a barrier that no preacher of hate will be able to scale for the foreseeable future. Let someone start attacking people for the fact of their difference in the years ahead, and someone else will remind them that our enemies make no such distinction.

## FREE TO BE

But surely, it will be said, the United States has responded by going to war, and war is harmful to the exercise of civil liberty. At one level, this is obviously true: Depending on how we pursue this war, we can expect pressure on newspapers to support their government, accusations against dissenters that they are aiding and abetting our enemies, and greater suspicion of those whose appearance or language marks them as somehow "different." Those who fear a potential encroachment on civil liberties can point to legislation that loosens restrictions on wiretapping and allows police and the courts to rely on foreign evidence gathered by means that did not meet U.S. constitutional standards. Yet the fact is that Congress raised serious questions about the administration's more draconian original proposals, reminding everyone of why we insist on the importance of civil liberties in the first place. There is no reason to believe that a U.S.–led campaign against terrorism will make such extensive inroads into civil liberties that anything like a police state will result.

There are two additional reasons why we are unlikely to see substantial encroachments on freedom as we mobilize for a response to terror. The first is that America has become a much more tolerant society than it was throughout most of the twentieth century. It was not that long ago when, in response to World War I, we banned the teaching of German in our schools or when, during the next world war, we locked up people who shared the same heritage—Japanese—as the enemy we were fighting. Nor can it easily be forgotten that, during the McCarthy period, we practiced a politics of intolerance that stigmatized the guilty and the innocent alike. The periods of intolerance that have marked our past have raised legitimate questions about how we will respond in the future.

Yet how we have changed! In interviews I have conducted with middle-class people from every corner of the United States, I have seen that a culture of nonjudgmentalism has become widespread in this country. With the exception of homosexuality and, to a lesser degree, illegal immigration, Americans seem increasingly reluctant to insist that certain ways of life are wrong, cruel, sinful, or misguided. Such non-judgmentalism can have its downside; as the terrorist attacks remind us, there are times when we need to insist that some kinds of acts are so evil that no excuse or justification for them is possible. But this particular variant of nonjudgmentalism has made few appearances in the aftermath of the attacks. Except for a few isolated voices on the left who found moral equivalence between the destruction of the World Trade Center and events such as the U.S. invasion of Grenada, most people in this country made the snap, and quite correct, judgment that the perpetrators of such evil acts can and ought to be punished for their deeds.

There is also a positive side to nonjudgmentalism: Compared to intolerance, it allows people to find the good among the bad. That may be why we are not likely to enter a new McCarthy period in the wake of the terrorist attacks despite the fact that most of the terrorists entered this country surreptitiously and that their religion is one that historically has fought wars against both Christians and Jews. It is true that in the days immediately following the attacks, incidents of hatred were directed not only against Muslims but also against others, such as Sikhs, who were mistaken for Muslims. There are no excuses for such deplorable acts. Yet they were not contagious; nothing in the response of the American people suggests anything like a hysterical, panic-driven movement to find scapegoats and hold them responsible. September 11 was not Pearl Harbor, and we are no longer the country of the Ku Klux Klan.

Another reason exists for concluding that a war against terror will fail to result in a serious diminution of civil liberty. Past wars, for all the restrictions on free speech they brought, also significantly expanded other kinds of liberty. Before World War II, America had no modern welfare state, and individuals had few protections against corporate power. In part because war demands that all those recruited to fight it be at the peak of physical and mental health, World War II, even more than the Great Depression, modernized the American state. Once the war was over and the troops returned home, no one could make the case that veterans did not deserve access to housing through a subsidized mortgage program, to education through the GI Bill, or to health care or death benefits. One of the effects of the war was to lift an entire generation of Americans into the ranks of the middle class and, by doing that, to expand their opportunities and those of their children. Despite the

subsequent election of conservative presidents such as Dwight Eisen-
hower, Richard Nixon, and Ronald Reagan in the decades after the war,
Republicans chose not to stop the expansion of government that the
war started. It is fair to say that the old isolationist and small-
government right wing never really survived World War II.

## CIVIC REENGAGEMENT

One of the unanswered questions stemming from the September 11
attacks is whether Americans will return to the culture of civic disengagement and disinterest that, according to critics such as Harvard political sci-
entist Robert Putnam, has characterized U.S. society since the passing of
more civic-minded generations. In some ways, the question answers itself.
If rates of participation and involvement do in fact vary with generations,
then the generation that will deal with the aftermath of September 11 is
also the generation that will change the most. Americans in their twenties
and thirties have never experienced recession or a war that threatened
their homeland. Now they are getting both at the same time. That may be
enough to shift their attention from dot-com start-ups to blood donation.
Who, after all, would have thought that there would be more Americans
prepared to help the injured than there were injured? Yet there were, and
not only because the sheer violence of the attack left so few survivors but
also because those who survived wanted to do something, anything, to
help. Americans went in a flash from bowling alone to surviving together.

It is also unlikely that one aspect of the recent civic disengagement—
a tendency to ignore anything that takes place outside U.S. borders—will
be sustainable in the aftermath of the attacks. As the president brings
more foreign leaders to the White House and travels around the world in
search of new partners, Americans will inevitably find themselves learning more about other countries and how their citizens view the world. No
one at this point can predict how forceful and persistent the American
response to terror will be. But it is not hard to predict that America will
be more engaged with the rest of the world than it has been for the past
two or three decades.

War cannot cure any of the pathologies that afflict the country. If Americans have lost the sense of moral wholeness that conservatives believe

they once possessed, they are unlikely to recover it just because some of their fellow citizens will be called on to sacrifice their comforts, and perhaps their lives, to combat terrorism. America may give too much to rich white males and too little to women and people of color, as many on the left charge, but neither the attacks themselves nor the responses to them will eliminate inequality and privilege. Then again, perhaps America was never in quite as bad shape as many of its critics suggested. To be sure, its moral condition has changed, just as its civic life has. But such changes have always been part of American history. And they rarely go only in one direction or only at one pace. If the attacks and their aftermath have effects on American civic culture, those effects are likely to be gradual rather than dramatic. They will take the form of reminders: suggestions that there are good reasons to be concerned with public life and warnings not to turn our backs on the needs of our fellow citizens.

Public life in the aftermath of September 11 will have its frustrations and restraints. We may never be able to stop terrorists from doing what they do. Americans may never get used to the new restrictions on the freedom to travel where and when we want. Political leaders may start looking for new moral campaigns at roughly the same time that economic leaders start putting profit first. Yet some aspects of the country's public life will be better for having lived through the attacks of September 11. Before that day, the American political system, for all its faults, guaranteed a level of personal freedom and democratic stability rare anywhere in this world. That has not changed and will not change because some fanatics hate us so much for doing so many things so well. If the tragedy generates a moment to pause and to reflect on who we are as a people and how we have changed from the days when we wrongly believed that the world's problems would never affect us, we will have matured as a nation.

## NOTE

This chapter is reprinted from *How Did This Happen?* by James F. Hoge Jr., ed., and Gideon Rose, ed. Copyright © 2001 by the Council on Foreign Relations, Inc. Reprinted by permission of Public Affairs, a member of Perseus Books, L.L.C.

## 20

# THE NEW PUBLIC SPIRIT

## Bruce J. Schulman

The federal government took over airline security and asserts new powers to secure the American "homeland." Outgoing New York Mayor Rudolph Giuliani pledged that rebuilding plans for the World Trade Center would center around a "soaring monument" to those who perished at the site. Despite heightened security, record crowds filled the streets to cheer on runners in the New York City Marathon and to celebrate First Night in Boston. Meanwhile, plans for a "faith-based" initiative to turn over provision of social services to religious institutions and a fiscal stimulus emphasizing tax reduction stalled in Congress.

Within months after the attacks of September 11, Americans were renegotiating the social contract, groping toward new understandings of national community. Over the past twenty-five years, Americans largely stressed the market and the private sphere over collective action, religious commitments over secular community, and individual rights over civic obligation. While it is too soon to draw definitive conclusions, the nation appears to have embarked in a different, more communitarian direction—rethinking the rights and the responsibilities of citizenship.

## TRAUMA AS CATALYST

Of course, war and national trauma always redefine American society, often in ways that do not become apparent until years after the crisis has passed. Six years of Franklin D. Roosevelt's New Deal barely relieved the poverty and misery of the Great Depression, but the collective effort altered the fundamental relations between state and society. It established the Social Security system, made organized labor a full partner in American public life, and brought immigrant Catholics and Jews into the counsels of power and the corridors of culture.

World War II similarly reknit the fabric of American life. The stunning success of the top secret Manhattan Project gave science new prestige and authority. It forged an alliance between government, universities, and research laboratories that still defines the scientific enterprise today and that no one could have predicted on the morning of Pearl Harbor.

Even more telling, World War II unleashed the civil rights revolution of the 1950s and 1960s. Military service created a cadre of activists and leaders—veterans who returned to the segregated South unwilling to accept the injustice they had fought to eradicate on the battlefield. Although not immediately apparent, the war against Fascism thoroughly undermined the idea of racial segregation. After the "final solution," notions of racial hierarchy, the very idea of fixed racial differences at all, became unacceptable. Before World War II, most Americans, even most liberals, believed racial justice an unrealizable goal and an unnecessary distraction from more serious reform. After World War II, civil rights reached the top of the policy agenda; President Harry Truman felt obliged to take steps, such as the desegregation of the armed forces, that his predecessor thought impossible.

Over a year after September 11, the implications of the current crisis are beginning to emerge. While it is too soon to know for sure, a number of trends point toward a new vision of community: secular, public spirited, and oriented more toward social responsibility than individual rights.

## PUBLIC OFFICIALS AND PUBLIC SPACES

First, as many observers have noted, the crisis has arrested the long-standing drift toward smaller government and privatization. Since the late 1960s, Americans have relied more heavily on the market to ensure prosperity and solve social problems. Even though they embraced specific public programs, Americans spoke derisively of government, nearly always referring to it in the third person as a hostile "they," never as the instrument of "our" national purpose. Amid the booming 1990s, Democrat Bill Clinton echoed the pronouncements of Republicans Richard Nixon and Ronald Reagan that the era of big government had ended.

Since September 11, long-scorned public institutions—Congress, the Pentagon, and even the Post Office—have become potent symbols of American democracy. Public employees have emerged as heroes, while private contractors no longer seem an efficient, reliable alternative to costly government agencies. Few Americans today prefer Argenbright Security to a public agency staffed by civil servants. To be sure, President George W. Bush has only reluctantly embraced the revival of the public sphere. His economic stimulus proposal would have stripped funds from initiatives not directly connected with the war on terrorism and shrunk government's capacity to take collective action in the future. But that program did not win congressional approval.

Americans have not only reconsidered the role of public institutions but have also taken to the nation's streets despite continued concerns about security. Indeed, the outpouring of assemblies in public spaces—vigils, marches, athletic events, concerts, charitable functions, and holiday celebrations—goes beyond a defiant response to the terrorist attacks. Rather, it suggests a new understanding of the need to build civic community outside the home and the marketplace, to reclaim and rebuild genuine public spaces. Americans seek settings for informal social interaction and democratic exchange.

This vibrant street life suggests a reversal of the nation's dependence on quasi-public spaces, such as privately owned and operated shopping malls, hotel atria, and commercial complexes connected by skyways and underground tunnels. Over the past three decades, the United States witnessed a thoroughgoing privatization of everyday life. Corporations and private organizations gradually assumed control over the basic services Americans relied on, the spaces where they congregated, and even the nation's hallowed instruments of self-rule. These facilities served some of the purposes of sidewalks, town squares, parks, and community centers, but lacked the openness, spontaneity, and potential for social interaction and community.

As Americans strolled through the overhead skyway or the upscale galleria, actual physical contact between different types of people diminished—between people of different ethnic and racial backgrounds, different lifestyles, different tastes and values, and different economic status. A sense of togetherness, of shared national identity, slowly atrophied. Malls and other private spaces regulated not only the climate but also the nature, appearance, and business practices of their tenants. They policed common spaces even more strictly, fixing seating and traffic patterns and manipulating music and climate controls to encourage consumption and influence patrons' behavior. Private security forces removed vagrants, quieted boisterous teens, and harassed loiterers. Unlike downtowns or city plazas, enclosed emporia guaranteed that their favored clientele would mix only with the right type of people. Even the newest megamalls, which serve a wide variety of people, began carefully monitoring patronage and segmenting areas of the mall by demographic groups.

Still, a genuine hunger for public space persisted, a craving for the excitement of city streets and the shared experience of the town square. The renewed popularity of farmers' markets and coffeehouses, the efforts to design "pedestrian pockets" in suburbs and small towns, the construction of light rail and trolley lines, the efforts of advocacy groups such as New York's Project for Public Spaces in trying to revive streets and public parks—all these attested to a continuing desire for public places to walk, talk, eat, drink, garden, exercise, and discover oneself or other people. The privatization of everyday life depleted America's stock of responsive, democratic, meaningful public space but never entirely erased the nation's desire to rediscover and resuscitate it.

The debate over the rebuilding of lower Manhattan has highlighted a renewed concern about democratic public space. Some voices argued that the World Trade Center site be left to market forces; initially, even Rudy Giuliani endorsed this view. But the former mayor and many others have since joined a consensus, one insisting that the site encourage commerce and reflection, that it include memorials and space for social interaction and civic purpose. The site of the demolished towers may suggest a new model of communitarian public space for the country.

## RELIGION AND RIGHTS

This revived community will surely be secular rather than religious. To be sure, the immediate aftermath of September 11 featured overt displays of faith. Churches from St. Paul's across the street from ground zero to the National Cathedral in Washington, where President Bush led a prayer service a few days after the attacks, played leading roles in the work of grief, relief, and community endeavor.

Still, the war on terrorism must prompt a rethinking of religion's place in the American public sphere. In past decades, religion has played an increasingly large role in public policy and social life. Public figures, even political leaders, have made open show of their spiritual beliefs, and the courts have relaxed the walls between church and state. President Bush's "faith-based initiative" proposed to turn provision of social services over to religious agencies. Even the recent vogue of John Adams, the intensely religious founding father who has replaced the Deist skeptic Thomas Jefferson in the national pantheon, testifies to a general comfort with overt displays of spirituality and a corresponding suspicion of people who do not avow religious faith.

But the national community, defined more by the flag than the cross since September 11, will likely insist on a more circumspect role for religion. Our war against terrorism—a war waged against a theocratic regime, terrorism inspired by religious beliefs—will necessarily prompt Americans to rethink the social and political influence of religion and perhaps to rebuild the barriers separating church and state. Certainly, the faith-based initiative will not proceed without much stronger safeguards.

Finally, public support for a reasonable middle ground on antiterrorism measures suggests a growing suspicion of excessive claims of individual rights. Despite the efforts of some partisans to frame the debate as a struggle between public safety and civil liberties, most Americans have remained sanguine, sensing the need for greater surveillance and security while remaining sensitive to the rights of minorities and individuals. In the process, many observers have pointed away from adversarial litigation as a vehicle for public policy and toward a more communitarian recognition of the obligations and the benefits of citizenship.

Making his farewell a few blocks from ground zero, Mayor Giuliani quoted from Lincoln's Gettysburg Address, the memorable oration that dedicated a blood-soaked battlefield to those who gave their lives that the nation might live. Lincoln saw in that tragedy the potential for "a new birth of freedom,"[1] the reestablishment of a union more generous, more responsible, more perfect than the noble experiment that had preceded it. Perhaps, as he surveyed the wreckage of September 11, the mayor saw it too.

## NOTES

This chapter was originally published in *The Responsive Community* 12, no. 2 (spring 2002): 30–35.

1. Abraham Lincoln, "Address at Gettysburg, Pennsylvania," *Abraham Lincoln: Speeches and Writings 1859–1865*, ed. Don E. Fehrenbacher (New York: Library of America, 1989), 536.

# GOVERNMENT TO THE RESCUE

## Albert R. Hunt

**A**s America fights a war on terrorism while celebrating heroism—especially that of our brave firemen, policemen, and emergency workers (public employees, one and all)—it's time to declare a moratorium on government bashing.

For a quarter century, the dominant public culture has suggested government is more a problem than a solution. Even in the most prosperous of times, pressures persisted to hold down spending; Democrats such as Bill Clinton and Al Gore bragged about cutting bureaucrats, and, until recently, regulation was a dirty word in the Bush administration. But, as during previous catastrophes, America turns to government in crisis. "We come to understand there are some things that only government can do," notes Senator John Kerry. "Our lives will be spent on a function a lot of people have made political meat out of cheapening and denigrating."

For the foreseeable future, the federal government is going to invest or spend more, regulate more, and exercise more control over our lives.

## MORE SPENDING, MORE REGULATION

That spending will change has been evident since the attack. As a percentage of the gross domestic product, federal spending has plummeted to 18.2 percent, the lowest level in thirty-five years. That trend will be dramatically reversed—some estimates put additional new spending at more than $1 trillion over the next several years—with vastly higher expenditures for the Pentagon, domestic security, failing industries, and the struggles of ordinary citizens.

These are the big-ticket items. But there are countless other claims, ranging from belatedly following the recommendations of Admiral William Crowe to spend an additional $1.4 billion a year to make American embassies safer, to hiring lots more Arabic language analysts and translators, to more money for public health.

But just as important as increased spending will be the need for more regulation. We will hear much less about the glories of privatization, as we have already in areas such as airport security. "Any debate about the federal role here is antique," asserted California Representative Jane Harman, the vice chair of the House Committee on Terrorism. "We know airport security has to be primarily a federal function." (The argument for arming pilots is insane, but the idea of armed air marshals is not. The government also needs to look at Vietnam-era technology that would permit pilots to automatically switch control of the plane to a ground controller in the event of an attempted hijacking.)

Top Bush administration officials will have to dramatically alter their views on regulation. The president has moved to crack down on resources available to terrorists, freezing their assets and warning foreign banks to cooperate by providing necessary records. Yet for all this, the Bush administration fought against tougher money-laundering regulations pushed by its predecessors and by the Organization for Economic Cooperation and Development. As late as July 2001, Treasury Secretary Paul O'Neill opposed any assault on money-laundering tax havens, questioning the United States' "right to tell other countries" what to do. Larry Lindsey, the White House's top economic official, privately met with lobbyists who were trying to kill any crackdown on money laundering.

## CAPITAL CONCERNS

A terrorist reliance on a system of informal, private transactions—called *hawala*—will enable them to escape some added scrutiny. The September 11 attacks may have been financed so cheaply—by some accounts it

cost as little as $200,000—that they didn't even require the use of fi-
nancial institutions and money laundering.

Yet, says Jack Blum, a Washington attorney and former congressional
investigator who for years has warned about terrorism, "money laundering is a big factor with these groups. It is essential to use government resources to stop it." Similarly, Senator Kerry notes that "*hawala* can never
make up for all terrorists' transfers through the [banking] system in
money laundering." A decade ago, the Massachusetts Democrat led a
congressional probe of the outlaw BCCI bank, through which Osama
bin Laden had laundered money.

Similarly, a left–right coalition has tried to deny access to U.S. capital
markets to oil companies doing business with Sudan. That country has harbored terrorists, including bin Laden, and used oil proceeds to wage geno-
cide on dissidents, killing two million. But the Bush administration fought
this measure as an unhealthy precedent for government intrusion. Any full-
scale war on terrorism must cut off from U.S. financial markets any countries or companies that traffic with terrorists or support terrorists.

To be sure, there always are dangers in bigger government. Congress
and the press must play a critical oversight role. It will be easy to reach
a consensus on denying capital markets to those who traffic with terrorists. But the concern posed earlier by Alan Greenspan and others of
runaway controls against anyone indirectly associated with drug dealers,
human rights violators, or countries whose policies we simply don't like
is substantive.

Tougher security measures at home are unavoidable. But liberals such
as Ralph Neas have justifiably questioned whether Attorney General John
Ashcroft has overreached in seeking unlimited detention of noncitizens or
expanded electronic surveillance in areas not related to terrorism. Before
granting vastly expanded powers, conservatives should ask a simple question: Would they give such authority to Bill Clinton or Janet Reno?

But there is no real debate over expansion in general. September 11
has underscored the centrality of government in our lives.

## NOTE

This chapter originally appeared in the *Wall Street Journal*, September 27,
2001, A19.

# INDEX

# ABOUT THE CONTRIBUTORS

**David Cole** is a professor at Georgetown University Law Center, the legal affairs correspondent for *The Nation,* and a volunteer staff attorney with the Center for Constitutional Rights. He is the author of *No Equal Justice: Race and Class in the American Criminal Justice System* and coauthor, with James X. Dempsey, of *Terrorism and the Constitution: Sacrificing Civil Liberties in the Name of National Security.* He has litigated a number of major First Amendment cases, including *Texas v. Johnson* (1989); *United States v. Eichman* (1990), which established that the First Amendment protects flag burning; and *National Endowment for the Arts v. Finley* (1998), which challenged the constitutionality of content restrictions on federal art funding.

**John Derbyshire**, a *National Review* contributing editor, has worked as a freelance journalist in the United Kingdom, the United States, and the Far East since 1983. The author of a novel, *Seeing Calvin Coolidge in a Dream,* he is currently engaged in writing a history and explanation of the Riemann hypothesis. Mr. Derbyshire was born in Northampton, England, but is now a U.S. citizen.

**Amitai Etzioni** is University Professor and the director of the Institute for Communitarian Policy Studies at The George Washington University.

He is the author of twenty-one books, including, most recently, *The Monochrome Society*, *Next: The Road to the Good Society*, and *The Limits of Privacy*. Professor Etzioni served as senior adviser to the White House from 1979 to 1980 and as president of the American Sociological Association from 1994 to 1995 and founded the International Society for the Advancement of Socio-Economics. He is the editor of *The Responsive Community*, a communitarian quarterly.

**Paul Glastris** is the editor-in-chief of the *Washington Monthly* and a senior fellow at the Western Policy Center in Washington, D.C. From September 1998 to January 2001, he was a special assistant and senior speechwriter to President Bill Clinton, in which capacity he cowrote the president's address to the Democratic convention in Los Angeles in August 2000 and contributed to his 1999 and 2000 State of the Union addresses. Before joining the White House, Glastris spent ten years as a correspondent and editor at *U.S. News & World Report*.

**Albert R. Hunt** is the executive editor of the *Wall Street Journal's* Washington bureau. He is the coauthor of *The American Elections of 1980*, *The American Elections of 1982*, *The American Elections of 1984*, and *Elections American Style*. Hunt is also a periodic panelist on NBC's *Meet the Press*. For seven years, he was a panelist on Public Broadcasting Service's *Washington Week in Review*, and he has been a member of the Cable News Network's *Capital Gang* since its inception in 1988.

**Michael Kinsley** is the founding editor of *Slate* (www.slate.com), an online magazine published by Microsoft Corporation. He is also a contributing writer at *Time*, and his weekly column appears in the *Washington Post*. Previously, he was cohost of the Cable News Network program *Crossfire*. Kinsley served two four-year stints as editor of *The New Republic*. He also has been editor of *Harper's* magazine, managing editor of the *Washington Monthly*, American Survey editor of *The Economist*, and a columnist for the *Wall Street Journal*. His writing has appeared in *The New Yorker*, *Condé Nast Traveler*, *Vanity Fair*, *Reader's Digest*, and other publications.

**Douglas W. Kmiec** is the dean and St. Thomas More Professor of Law at the Catholic University of America in Washington, D.C. Dean Kmiec came to CUA after having taught constitutional law for nearly two decades at the University of Notre Dame and being the inaugural holder of the Caruso Family Endowed Chair at Pepperdine University in California. The coauthor of *The American Constitutional Order* and numerous other scholarly books and articles, he served Presidents Ronald Reagan and George H. W. Bush during 1985–1989 as constitutional legal counsel—assistant attorney general, Office of Legal Counsel, U.S. Department of Justice—a position previously held by Chief Justice William Rehnquist and Justice Antonin Scalia.

**Mark Krikorian** is executive director of the Center for Immigration Studies, a nonprofit, nonpartisan research organization in Washington, D.C., that examines and critiques the impact of immigration on the United States. Krikorian frequently testifies before Congress and has published articles in the *Washington Post*, the *New York Times*, *Commentary*, *National Review*, and elsewhere and has appeared on *60 Minutes, Nightline*, the *NewsHour with Jim Lehrer*, Cable News Network, National Public Radio, and many other television and radio programs.

**Michael Lind** is a senior fellow at the New America Foundation. He has previously been an editor or staff writer for *The New Yorker, Harper's* magazine, and *The National Interest.* Lind's three books of political journalism and history—*The Next American Nation, Up from Conservatism,* and *Vietnam*—were all selected as *New York Times* Notable Books of the Year. His most recent book is *The Radical Center,* coauthored with Ted Halstead.

**John McCain** is a U.S. senator from Arizona. Senator McCain was first elected to represent the state of Arizona in the U.S. House of Representatives in 1982. He served two terms in the House before being elected to the Senate in 1985. Senator McCain has received numerous awards from taxpayer and foreign policy organizations for his public service. In 1997, he was named one of the "25 Most Influential People in America" by *Time* magazine. The son and grandson of prominent Navy admirals, Senator McCain began a twenty-two-year career as a naval aviator after graduating from the U.S. Naval Academy in 1958.

His naval honors include the Silver Star, Bronze Star, Legion of Merit, Purple Heart, and Distinguished Flying Cross. His memoir, *Faith of My Fathers,* detailing his early life and military career, spent twenty-four weeks on the *New York Times* best-seller list. Senator McCain has seven children and four grandchildren. He and his wife, Cindy, reside in Phoenix.

**Richard A. Posner** is a judge of the U.S. Court of Appeals for the Seventh Circuit and was chief judge of the court from 1993 to 2000. He is also a senior lecturer at the University of Chicago Law School. Judge Posner has written many influential books on law and legal theory, including *Economic Analysis of Law, The Problematics of Moral and Legal Theory,* and *Antitrust Law.* His most recent book is *Public Intellectuals: A Study of Decline.*

**Steven V. Roberts** is the Shapiro Professor of Media and Public Affairs at The George Washington University, where he teaches a course on the media's role in the public policy process. His journalistic career of almost forty years has included assignments as both White House and congressional correspondent for the *New York Times.* With his wife, Cokie Roberts, he wrote *From This Day Forward,* a national bestseller about marriage in America.

**Bruce J. Schulman** is director of American studies and professor of history at Boston University. He is the author of three books—*From Cotton Belt to Sunbelt, Lyndon B. Johnson and American Liberalism,* and *The Seventies: The Great Shift in American Culture, Politics, and Society*—the last of which the *New York Times* named one of its Notable Books of the Year for 2001. A frequent contributor to the *New York Times,* the *Los Angeles Times,* and numerous other publications, Schulman has held research fellowships from the National Endowment for the Humanities and the Charles Warren Center for Studies in American History, among many others.

**Laurence H. Tribe** is the Tyler Professor of Constitutional Law at Harvard Law School. He has written the leading modern treatise on the U.S. Constitution and many other books and articles. Tribe holds six honorary degrees, is the leading academic who is also a frequent advocate in the U.S. Supreme Court, was voted best Harvard Law School professor in 2001, and won the New York University Annual Survey of Law Award in 2002 (previously awarded to George Mitchell, Desmond Tutu, and such U.S. Supreme Court justices as William Brennan, Thurgood Marshall, Harry Blackmun, John Paul Stevens, Sandra Day O'Connor, and Ruth Bader Ginsburg).

**Alan Wolfe** is professor of political science and director of the Boisi Center for Religion and American Public Life at Boston College. He is the author or editor of more than ten books, including *Marginalized in the Middle* and *One Nation, After All.* His most recent book is *Moral Freedom: The Search for Virtue in a World of Choice.* Both *One Nation, After All* and *Moral Freedom* were selected as *New York Times* Notable Books of the Year. A contributing editor of *The New Republic* and *The Wilson Quarterly,* Wolfe writes often for those publications as well as for *Commonweal,* the *New York Times, Harper's* magazine, *The Atlantic Monthly,* the *Washington Post,* and other magazines and newspapers.

**C. Robert Zelnick** spent twenty-one years with ABC News, including eight as a Pentagon correspondent. He has won two Emmy awards and two Gavel awards for his reporting. He is the author of three books, including a biography of Al Gore and, most recently, *Winning the Florida Election: How the Bush Team Fought the Battle.* A graduate of Cornell University and the University of Virginia Law School, he is currently the chairman of the Department of Journalism at Boston University and a research fellow at the Hoover Institution.